The Bootstrap Entrepreneur

The Bootstrap Entrepreneur

STEVEN C. BURSTEN

THOMAS NELSON PUBLISHERS
Nashville

Published in Nashville, Tennessee, by Oliver-Nelson Books, a division of Thomas Nelson, Inc., Publishers, and distributed in Canada by Lawson Falle, Ltd., Cambridge, Ontario.

Except where indicated, names and events have been fictionalized to protect privacy.

Printed in the United States of America.

Library of Congress Cataloging-in-Publication Data

Bursten, Steven C., 1937–
    The bootstrap entrepreneur / Steven C. Bursten.
       p. cm.
    Includes bibliographical references.
    ISBN 0-8407-9185-2 (pbk.)
    1. New business enterprises—Management. 2. Small business—Management. I. Title.
    HD62.5.B84 1993
    658.4'21—dc20   93-18264
                                        CIP

1 2 3 4 5 6 — 98 97 96 95 94 93

To Valerie,
my marriage and business partner
for twenty-nine years.
Her wittiness makes marriage fun,
and her gentle, insightful inspiration
brings out the best in all.
I owe her special thanks for her brilliance
in coining
Bootstrap Entrepreneur.

and

In memory of Morris Bursten,
my dear, sweet father
whose kindness and service to others
lighted an example
not only for the families close to him
but as the founding philosophy for over
one thousand caring Decorating Den franchise owners.
May his soul gently touch
every reader of this book.

Contents

In Tribute

This book is in tribute to the 15 million wonderful men and women who struggle every day in the jungle of competitive pressures trying to do their level best to please and serve their customers. They are good people, dedicated to giving what no major corporation can equal—heart, soul, and lifetime personal commitment to building friends in their community and turning friends into customers. At the same time, they strive to build a prosperous business for themselves and their families.

They receive no government handouts. They are too naive and too religious to give less than a full measure of integrity. They are too unschooled to manipulate a leveraged buyout (LBO) or an employee stock option plan (ESOP). But they know how to stand responsible for their decisions, to fill six different job descriptions every day, and to wake up each morning with unbridled optimism that the future will be better than the past.

Further warm thoughts are extended to the millions of men and women who will risk venturing into a new business this and every year. And to the millions more who dream of the day they will join other Bootstrap Entrepreneurs in taking control of their future.

It is you, the American pioneers of the 1990s, whom *The Bootstrap Entrepreneur* is intended to serve.

In Appreciation

A sincere thank you to business associates, good friends, and family who encouraged me over the years, and most especially to those kind souls who took time from their busy lives to read and comment on this book to make it even more useful to the reader: Jim Bailey; Richard Cahill; Leonard Casey; Bill Cherkasky; Dr. Phillip Cohen; Douglas Decker, Ph.D.; Raymond J. Groll; Ira Hayes; David Heilwagen; Jim Hendricks; Deborah Hitchcock; Danielle Kennedy; Rod Kramer; Reva Lesonsky; Mamie McCullough; Jim McGrath; Joann McVay; John Mandeville; Dr. Robert Mercer; Sharon Nelton; Harvey Nudelman; Gary Ruben; Charles Slater; Maurice Stans; and to loving family members, sons David and Eric, Aunt Frieda, my mother, Dee, and of course, Valerie.

How This Book Is Organized

Part 1: What's Ahead? Part 2: Business Baloney	Introduction and orientation to owning and operating your own business
↓	
Part 3: Why Be a Bootstrap Entrepreneur?	Is business ownership right for you? Thoughts, perspectives, and self-test
↓	
Part 4: Choosing Your Business Part 5: Checking Out the Business You Like	Choosing your business and checking it out—ideas, insights, and how-to-do-it instructions
↓	
Part 6: Get Ready Part 7: Get Set	Planning and preparation—mission, purpose, values, and detailed nitty-gritty
↓	
Part 8: Secrets of Starting on a Shoestring	Time out! What to do if your cash is limited but your confidence and enthusiasm aren't
↓	
Part 9: Go! Part 10: Looking Back	Essentials and attitudes to succeed as you start; how you'll feel three years later

Part 1

What's Ahead?

Chapter 1

Why Read This Book?

First and foremost, this book will help you decide if you should even consider the idea of independent business ownership.

If your decision is yes, it will guide you to narrow your options of businesses, looking to your strengths and interests as a starting point.

Next, it will explain how to do it so you invest the least money and hit a break-even point quickly.

Finally, once you're up and running, it will help you maximize your financial opportunities down the road.

The bottom line reasons to read this book are to invest thousands less in getting a business started, to sell thousands more your first year, and to keep thousands of dollars in extra profits for yourself.

Beneficial Tips

Keep a notebook or steno pad handy. Every Bootstrap Entrepreneur I know uses a planning notebook and calendar. Start a section on ideas for your new business.

Next, you'll notice a lot of white space in this book. It's intentional. Make notes as you go. Books are not sacred. They're meant to be scribbled in (if they're your books). No scribbly notes means a book wasn't very interesting and didn't stimulate many ideas. What a waste of your time! You will benefit by your great ideas that flash in your mind as you read.

Chapter 2

Who Is This Book For?

This book is not written for Harvard MBA graduates. It is not intended for Silicon Valley computer wizards harnessing a technological breakthrough. It is not for engineers or research scientists who developed a new process for gene splicing or releasing energy by cold fusion.

Instead, this book is for persons who want to take control of their lives, persons who have been working for others too long, persons who dream that somehow, someway, someday, they will work for themselves. They want to own a business, to stand or fall by their own merit.

This book is for people who want a challenge, who want to build something for their future and for their family's future, who want to do the kind of work they enjoy and believe in. These people see themselves as doers more than supervisors, yet dream of the day when they will lead their own successful organizations.

Who Are They?

Who are these people? They are all around you, perhaps individuals much like you—former nurses, sales executives, frustrated office workers, airline pilots, teachers, fire fighters, homemakers, law enforcement officers, retired military personnel starting a second career, laid-off managers determined never again to let a corporation control their destiny, and on and on.

Could One of These Bootstrap Entrepreneurs Be You?

John was a twenty-three-year-old college student. Inspired by marketing courses to own a business, he began a window cleaning service with a friend for $2,000. Twelve years later, he continues and prospers.

Phyllis was a thirty-nine-year-old executive secretary. Conscientious and determined, she wanted to have a baby, stay home to raise him, but still contribute to the family income. With a borrowed $3,000, she bought a computer, a laser printer, and copy and fax machines, and she started an in-home secretarial service. In less than one year, she is booked solid with clients.

Bob was a top beautician who cared about his customers but wanted to work for himself. Rather than lose a good employee, his boss became Bob's partner in a successful new shop in a growing community.

Wanda was a dental hygienist whose children were grown. She had the option to choose home or career. Wanda wanted to learn and grow as an independent businessperson, so she invested $20,000 in a decorating franchise. Overwhelmed at first, she learned quickly, tried hard, and soon became a successful business leader in her community.

Bob W. retired in his fifties as a top marketing executive with a major chemical company. Along with his wife of thirty-five years, he started a custom closet business in a growing southwestern Florida community. Now Bob and

Ann are busy, successful, and enjoying the best years of their marriage.

Janet was a twenty-seven-year-old successful middle-management sales executive with a major West Coast firm. She was a hard worker and wanted to get ahead. Her ambition led her to try a part-time multilevel sales opportunity with an emerging national cosmetics firm. After a few months, she swallowed hard and cut the cord from her secure $50,000-a-year job to take her cosmetics business full-time. Now she's built a sales team of dozens of part-time and full-time distributors, and it's the best decision she ever made.

Rod was a twenty-six-year-old law enforcement officer, and before that, he was a leader in the army's crack Ranger unit. His physical strength, determination, and desire to control his own destiny led him to move to California and start an unusual mobile fitness business. Two years later, he was featured in the *Los Angeles Times,* and he is now adding a second truck and building an organization.

Two Things in Common?

Every one of these individuals is different, but each shares two things in common: each wanted to make a change, and each was willing to take a risk. In these challenging times, a lot of people want to make a change. What gave these people the courage to risk starting their own independent businesses?

That's what this book is all about—building courage and confidence to start your own business. Deep down, you have the desire, or you wouldn't be reading these words. In your case, perhaps you should start now, or maybe you should prepare yourself a while longer. When you finish these pages, you will know the answer, and you will know exactly what to do next. If you sincerely want the opportunity to make more money, to achieve financial independence today and in the future, if you want to make a change and need only the courage to take a risk, this book is for you.

Qualities of a Successful Bootstrap Entrepreneur

Dreams big dreams despite small pocketbook

- Is creative and resourceful
- Uses time and energy, not cash

Dares to take a risk

- Has the essence of entrepreneur spirit

Accepts responsibility

- Will stand on performance
- Does not blame others for setbacks

Seeks independence and control

- Wants freedom to make decisions
- Wants control over future
- Wants to make things better

Believes in self

- Strives for personal development
- Wants rewards for achievement
- Expects excellence from self and others

Wants to contribute

- Serves others
- Seeks good works above money
- Will go the extra mile

Chapter 3

Who Is a Bootstrap Entrepreneur?

A Bootstrap Entrepreneur is a person who has big dreams but a small pocketbook. A Bootstrap Entrepreneur is a new American pioneer, a self-reliant person who seeks freedom and control—just like the pioneers who built America. A Bootstrap Entrepreneur is defined by fear and ennobled by courage. While fearing failure, a Bootstrap Entrepreneur intuitively understands every person learns more from failure, seldom from success. Willingness to risk failure is the starting point for all growth and achievement.

. . . .

You have to be willing to lose in order to win.

. . . .

Bootstrap Entrepreneurs are all ages. Although two-thirds are under forty, one-tenth are over fifty. A Bootstrap Entrepreneur is any person who aspires to own or already owns a business. It is a salesperson who works on commission, a distributor in a network marketing organization. It is any person who knows that you must be willing to lose in order to win, that you can learn and benefit from every experience, and that freedom and financial independence in a business of your own are worth the price to be paid.

Diane Did It Right

Diane worked in a flower shop. She'd been there about two years, earning only enough for basics, supplemented with income from a divorce settlement. She liked the floral business, but soon she learned how the owner, Marjorie, struggled to pay rent, purchase supplies, meet the payroll and, of course, buy just the right amount of fresh flowers so she wouldn't miss any sales of what customers wanted, yet wouldn't have to throw away good money on blooms that lost their freshness.

Diane could do most of the jobs in the store and was pretty good at arranging flowers, although Marjorie was more experienced and more talented artistically. Diane most liked meeting the public and seeing each person's excitement with the beautiful arrangement or the surprise when she delivered an unexpected gift.

Diane noticed the store had all kinds of customers and sold flowers for all the usual occasions: weddings, graduations, funerals, dinners, and other events. She observed that many of the store's customers were from nearby businesses who called on the phone to order arrangements to give their clients as a thank-you or to recognize special achievements.

Diane also noticed that many businesses used flowers and plants to enhance the environment. Banks, medical offices, and some others liked freshly cut floral arrangements. Others, more budget conscious, used silk or plastic permanent arrangements.

Spotting an underserved potential need, or market niche as the experts call it, Diane asked her employer for permission to begin a part-time noncompetitive business serving business accounts that would not walk in to Marjorie's store.

Marjorie agreed to sell bulk flowers to Diane for 60 percent off the regular price and arrangements for 40 percent off. That way Marjorie still made 20 to 30 percent profit without any increase in overhead, labor, or advertising costs, and Diane didn't have to set up an account with wholesalers or purchase minimum amounts to qualify for a dealership status.

Diane named her small sideline business FLOWERS-TO-GO. She created a simple brochure suggesting all the ways a business could show appreciation. She asked questions of business owners to learn about people they wanted to recognize frequently, such as a top customer ranking each month or customers who purchased the most of a featured product. Another need was to recognize a top salesperson or clerk of the month. Then Diane negotiated unique floral arrangements, attractive pricing, and delivery to recognize the special people each month.

Next, Diane visited a high-quality silk flower retailer to set up a similar arrangement so that she could work off the inventory and still make a 40 percent profit margin. The profit was not as much as if she went direct to wholesalers, but Diane could afford to pay a little extra because her overhead costs were low and she needed more volume before going direct to wholesalers. With the option to offer fresh flowers or permanent arrangements, she encouraged her customers to spruce up their businesses to enhance the environment for employees and customers.

Within a few months Diane's business was thriving. She developed personal relationships with her customers—often sending flowers to their wives as a special surprise. She thanked them with follow-up notes. Every ninety days she sent out a friendly bulletin with interesting ideas about how to build business and keep customers by using fresh and permanent flowers.

Diane bought a minivan to make deliveries. She traded in her personal car, so the vehicle she drives every day is tax deductible. She painted a bold appealing sign on the van with her telephone number large and easy to read. Several weeks ago she found a housebound mother of two with a pleasing personality to answer her telephone and help with paperwork. All the essentials were in place—a company name, business cards, a business license, a bookkeeping system, a company vehicle, a business phone with a yellow page ad soon to appear, a friendly, reliable, and low-cost part-time employee able to work more as business expands. And most of all, Diane had a following of satisfied customers to buy more from her each month and refer her to others. Sales and profits were still skimpy, but trends were favorable. Diane decided to take the final scary step: leave her job at Marjorie's Flower Shop and go full-time to build her new business.

Bootstrap Entrepreneurs Get Customers First and Spend Money Later

Diane's story is a classic of how a Bootstrap Entrepreneur gets started with limited capital, yet can build a big business by finding customers first and avoiding substantial investments with costly mistakes.

Would you like to do what Diane did? Start on a shoestring and build a good business quickly? Well, I can't promise that every Bootstrap Entrepreneur who reads this book will become a Diane or sell $1 million the first year. But for sure, you can stack the deck in your favor. By combining your drive with my experience-tested principles, you can improve your odds.

Chapter 4

Why This Book Was Written

Guiding independent business owners to success is much like coaching a team to victory. For years, I have advised struggling new entrepreneurs who bootstrapped themselves to success in small business. Few satisfactions equal the pleasure of watching them grow. Like seeing your children become good citizens, it is a thrill to watch independent business owners mature and succeed.

Those wonderful men and women were from all walks of life. Some were from big corporations; some never held a job. Others were bookkeepers, engineers, medical technicians, dry cleaners, office supply salespersons, and many others from many occupations. Whatever their backgrounds, the men and women had dreams and the courage to start businesses. They wanted to stand on their own two feet, to build something for their future.

Seeing their vitality and enthusiasm as they started their businesses, and later their thrill as they succeeded, has been my driving force for a quarter century. I hope this book will bring the same growth and success to many more Bootstrap Entrepreneurs.

Chapter 5

A Quiet Note to Business Professionals

Experienced business executives may wonder why only limited financial planning is recommended for the Bootstrap Entrepreneur. That is a fair question. Obviously, any person planning a major business investment should put more emphasis in this area. Included would be a schedule of capital investment needs, inventory requirements, employee staffing, accrual and cash flow forecasts, and anticipated return on investment.

These issues are largely bypassed in this book for Bootstrap Entrepreneurs. Instead, a bias toward marketing and a focus on sales are given priority. Why?

The rationale is stated eloquently in the *Small Business Primer*, published by the NFIB Foundation, an affiliate of the National Federation of Independent Business: "It is difficult to over-emphasize the importance of sales to financial health and profitability of a business. . . . Without sales, there are no profits and without profits, there is no business."

According to this same report, of the more than 15 million nonfarm small businesses in America, over 80 percent

have fewer than five employees. The initial financial investment for one-third of these new business start-ups is less
than $10,000. And for three out of four, the investment is
under $50,000.

This study parallels my observations in talking to, and
working with, thousands of independent business owners in
my thirty-year business career. Accordingly, the capital and
staffing requirements for a Bootstrap Entrepreneur are mea-
surably different from those for a more sophisticated venture.

At the risk of oversimplification, I have tried to focus on
the issues that count the most to give the Bootstrap Entrepreneur the best chance to survive. Then as the business grows,
more attention will be given to business planning, break-
even analysis, and staffing needs.

Part 2

Business
Baloney

Chapter 6

Business
Baloney

In my first several years of calling on small businesses, I asked every owner I met, "What makes you successful?" It took hundreds of interviews to discover the truth:

1. Some business owners didn't know why they were successful.
2. Some owners thought they knew why, but they were often wrong.
3. Some owners were not successful at all. (But they always had advice for others.)

As a result, I came to learn that much of what we hear and read about business success is really worthless. So before we get started with ideas that work, I want to bury this useless advice I call *business baloneyisms*.

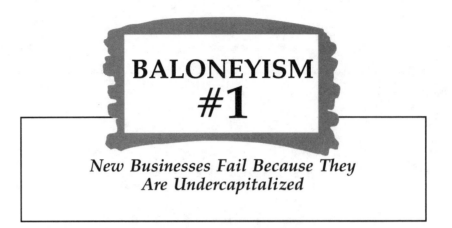

BALONEYISM #1

*New Businesses Fail Because They
Are Undercapitalized*

New businesses don't fail because they're short of money. They fail because they're short of customers. *Undercapitalized* simply means the money ran out before enough customers walked in. The number one rule for the Bootstrap Entrepreneur is: CUSTOMERS FIRST!

Jim's Paint and Wallpaper Store

Jim opened a paint and wallpaper store in a neighborhood shopping center in a growing southern community. He had been warned by his suppliers and similar business owners in other cities to avoid discounting. Give good service instead, and people will spread the word about you, they said. In the first two months, Jim took out a few large splashy newspaper ads. He got some customers but not enough to cover the advertising cost. Then he settled down to wait for the word to get around about his new store.

Jim busied himself rearranging displays, trimming windows, keeping the store clean, and lavishing extra service on every customer who walked in. Jim's customers liked him and generally came back. But he didn't have enough of them. Sixteen months after he opened, Jim closed the doors and folded the operation.

Undercapitalized?

Was Jim undercapitalized? No, the real culprit was something else. Jim lacked fierce determination to bring in customers no matter what. He could have watched the building permits section in the newspaper, then called people, mailed them fliers, and/or made a personal visit. He could have offered free remodeling and wallpapering clinics at his store and could have done lots of other things to stimulate sales. Unfortunately, even though he gave good service, Jim never really understood the first law of business: without customers, there is no business.

BALONEYISM #2

*You Have to Be a College Graduate
with Many Hours
of Business Courses*

Only about one-fifth of new business owners have college degrees. Over one-third have taken no business courses at all. Being a college graduate is certainly a plus, but it's not in any way a reason to wait before starting your business.

Desire Counts More Than a College Degree

Andy didn't have a college degree. He went to a trade school for woodworking and construction, then served as an apprentice carpenter in his early twenties. By age thirty, he was experienced in residential home building and remodeling. Personable and conscientious, Andy did high-quality work on time and within budget for his employer. He was often put in charge of projects and had many dealings with customers. Over the years, Andy was exposed to every aspect of the residential construction business and was well respected by the trade and the public.

As Andy's first child, Jennifer, turned two years old, his wife, Joan, was asked by her former boss to return to a supervisory position in a nearby manufacturing plant. Andy and Joan decided together that it was time for Andy to take the step he'd been wanting to take for years—start his own contracting business. If the family cut needs to the bare essentials, Joan's income would keep them going awhile.

Within four years, Andy became a leading home builder in his community. Andy isn't good at long-term cash analysis, and he doesn't personally understand all the complex tax and legal issues about his business. Nevertheless, he knows how to buy materials right and how to price new homes he builds so he makes a profit. For the more complicated matters, Andy hired the best independent CPA and one of the top lawyers in the area. Though they charged a bit more than others, their advice was worth it.

To further broaden himself, Andy joined a business executives club to meet and learn from other successful businesspeople. He also did a lot of reading and attended special seminars on supervisory practices and business operation whenever he could. As a member of the local and national homebuilders' association, Andy often attended training events and seminars it sponsored.

No, Andy didn't have a college education, but he had good horse sense, associated with successful business owners, hired the best expert talent, and constantly educated himself in what he needed to know to build a solid and successful contracting business.

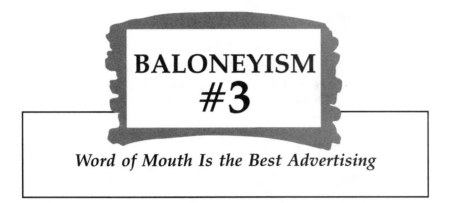

BALONEYISM #3

Word of Mouth Is the Best Advertising

For a new business, word of mouth is the worst advertising!

Why? Because it doesn't exist!

If you have a new business, no one knows who you are, no one knows the products you sell, and no one knows the services you offer. If no one knows you, there is no way to get word-of-mouth advertising.

Sure, word of mouth is the best advertising *after* you get established. But businesses that rely mainly on word-of-mouth advertising may take five years or more to build up.

The Bootstrap Entrepreneur doesn't have that much time!

Remember Jim?

Remember Jim's paint store from Baloneyism #1? He failed because he waited for word of mouth to feed him enough customers. It's too risky to wait. Start promoting from the first day. But don't blow the budget on a few big ads. Do little low-cost things every day to get the word out. In the beginning, you won't have many customers to take your time. That means you have time to make phone calls, write notes, and knock on doors, so do all three.

Sally Wouldn't Wait

Sally started a hair salon. She had a great location in a neighborhood shopping center. She also had a good following from four years as a stylist for another salon in the same city. Sally knew that the traffic passing by her shop on the way to other stores plus word-of-mouth advertising would probably be enough to cover operating expenses within a few months. But Sally was ambitious—she didn't want to wait forever to make high profits.

So Sally approached her accountant for advice to develop a sales projection. Together, they projected $110,000 the first year, $140,000 the second year, and $175,000 the third year. I suggested Sally try the formula in 44, "Marketing Plan," and set an advertising budget of 15 percent of her expected first-year sales.

Sally decided that with a strong advertising budget, she would sell $160,000 the first year, $210,000 the second year, and $280,000 the third year. With this approach she would invest $2,000 per month, or $24,000 for advertising for the first year.

An Extra $150,000 for Sally

Now here's the interesting part. Through strong advertising, Sally's sales were expected to increase the first year from $110,000 to $160,000—a difference of $50,000. Because she would spend almost half that amount, or $24,000, for advertising, there really would not be any added profit for her the first year (cost of products and stylists would take the rest). However, by the third year, the difference would be $105,000 more in sales, and the added profit would be at least $30,000 that year and each year for years to come.

Not only would each year be more profitable, but the business itself would have a higher market value if it were sold, especially with the good name established by a strong advertising budget. Over a five-year period, Sally expected to benefit by at least $150,000 in increased net profit and higher buildup of market value in her business. Sally didn't have a lifetime to wait for word-of-mouth advertising. She had high goals and belief in herself; she backed her belief with a strong advertising budget and built a better business faster.

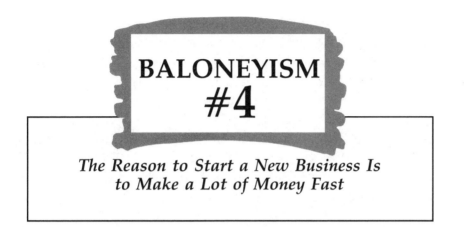

BALONEYISM #4

The Reason to Start a New Business Is to Make a Lot of Money Fast

Money is important, but greed is counterproductive. When you have dollar signs in your eyes, customers see them right away. Successful Bootstrap Entrepreneurs start a new business because they want to contribute something special to their customers—an extra edge the competition doesn't offer.

If you don't believe this, don't start a new business. If you do believe it—and do it—money will follow as quickly as you deserve it.

Serving Others Is the Key

Diane, who started the floral business, is a good example. She believed in her product (flowers and the pleasure they bring the person who receives them), and she believed business owners would benefit by using flowers to give recognition and appreciation. She sincerely wanted to serve customers and to have everyone benefit, flower givers and flower receivers alike. Helping everyone feel better and do better was number one. Then the money followed later.

Bill's Insurance Agency

Bill finished college and immediately joined an independent insurance agency. His dad was successful in his own agency before he died and the business was sold. Bill took extra courses in college so he would have a strong knowledge base to render professional service.

After working in the agency less than two years, Bill began to sense a difference between himself and the other representatives, even the owner. Bill wanted to build long-term relationships and referrals, not make big quick hits. That difference caused him to leave the agency and strike out on his own.

Builds Repeat and Referral Business

Bill was young, and many customers he served were young. He went out of his way to give them the best coverage possible for their pocketbooks. Bill used his college training and his experience to save money for his clients. Many times he could have made extra dollars by selling more than they needed, but he didn't. The result: a growing clientele of young people who grew and prospered. They kept Bill as their agent for life. The young people also referred Bill to their parents and relatives who had greater needs and a larger budget.

Because Bill went into business to serve his clients first and to think of his pocketbook second, he built a large agency in only a few years and actually earned much more money than others who had dollar signs in their eyes every time they met a customer.

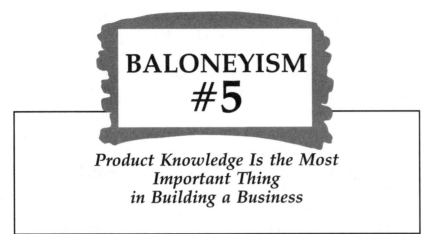

BALONEYISM #5

Product Knowledge Is the Most Important Thing in Building a Business

Most independent business owners are product focused. That's often why they start a business. The Bootstrap Entrepreneur is, on the other hand, customer focused and knows that customer knowledge is more important than product knowledge. It's amazing how much product you can sell with the knowledge you already have. Customers will tell you the products they need, the price they will pay, the delivery they expect, the performance they require . . . *if you listen!*

The Bootstrap Entrepreneur who uses listening skills, creativity, and questions while striving to become a product expert will discover that people knowledge is even more essential than product knowledge in building a business.

EZ Office Equipment, Inc.

Becky was new to office equipment sales. She recently started a new business, EZ Office Equipment, Inc., with her good friend Nadine, who for six years sold copy machines for a leading national manufacturer. Their idea was to get a toehold with a line of new imported copiers ideal for offices needing five thousand to seventy-five thousand copies per month. Next, they wanted to add computers, fax machines, and other items.

Their concept was to provide service to customers when they initially obtained equipment and also when a product malfunctioned. They helped each customer train new employees on equipment purchased or leased from EZ Office Equipment.

Becky and Nadine realized if they were to make money, both needed to promote new business. The challenge was how to get Becky to become an experienced professional in the shortest possible time and to provide proper guidance to customers.

Here's how they solved it. Becky's job was to call on new accounts but *not* to see the owner first. That approach was just the opposite of competitors who wanted to meet the decision maker immediately.

Instead, Becky's job was to meet the employees who actually needed photocopies. She explained to the employees that while she represented EZ Office Equipment, her real interest was to learn more about potential customers and their future needs for the next year or two.

Then she opened a notebook portfolio to record what the employees told her. Tucked inside the portfolio was a short checklist Becky referred to unobtrusively:

1. Number copies/month?
2. Who uses machine most?
3. Are copies used in office or out?
4. Two sides important?
5. Color important?
6. What is liked about present machine? What is disliked?
7. What features would be liked if available?
8. Any talk about needing new machine?
9. Monthly cost of old mach./maint.?
10. If we could get a new machine with added features you want but at below price now paying, might boss be interested?

When Becky found someone interested, she asked other questions as the interview developed. She made lots of notes. After fifteen to twenty minutes, she said, ''Thanks so much for the time you've taken. I don't know whether I can solve all the needs you've presented, but I have some ideas I think you'll like. For now, I want to take this information back to the office and carefully assess whether one of our copier models can do all you want within your company's budget.'' As she was leaving, Becky made a point to meet the owner to say hello and leave a favorable impression.

You can guess the rest. Becky went back to her office and met with Nadine. Together, they decided the best model and how to present it. But what if Becky didn't have a partner with lots of product knowledge? Chances are, someone could help her, such as a supplier or a friend. Becky would likely not get into a new business without knowing someone with the technical knowledge she needed. The point is, she didn't have to be the world's best expert. Becky needed only to ask customers what they did currently, what changes or differences they wanted, and what they liked or disliked about their present product (or competition). Then she could use the information to present a workable solution. The customers themselves would help Becky get the order because she *listened* and she *cared*.

BALONEYISM #6

You Can't Find Good Help

The real issue is not finding good help; it's finding good leaders! A good leader will attract good people. A leader will convince employees of their opportunity for a bright future. Good employees buy into great ideas, even more than great wages. Much of an employee's compensation is not just the paycheck but the opportunity to learn and grow. An ambitious apprentice will pay a master to learn new skills. If you're a masterful leader, you will find good people to share your dream and learn from you.

Arnold Recruits Rich

Arnold operated a shoe store in a neighborhood shopping center, selling quality upper-medium-price name brands. Competition from nearby shopping centers was intense, especially because multiple shoe stores in a mall create synergistic appeal of vast selection. Nevertheless, Arnold enjoyed an excellent reputation and a successful business.

Arnold relied on three key factors for success: (1) merchandise was carefully targeted in styling and value to the dense nearby neighborhoods; (2) everyday pricing was 15 to 20 percent less than shopping mall stores due to his lower overhead cost; and (3) Arnold, as an owner, was active and respected in the community. He contributed to charities, supplied shoes to school athletic teams, and served the well-being of the neighborhood every way possible.

As his business grew, Arnold wanted to add a salesperson. Because his was a small business, he couldn't afford corporate training programs, high wages, and extensive fringe benefits as some large chain shoe stores could. Nevertheless, Arnold recruited a crackerjack young man named Rich, who quickly endeared himself to established clientele. In a few months, sales and profits grew to their highest level ever for Arnold's business.

How did Arnold hire a better person for less money? It seems impossible, but here's what Arnold told Rich: "Look, Rich, I can't give you a lot of money at first. We've got to get higher sales to get you a higher income. And I can't give you all the fringes and fancy surroundings you might get at a mall store. But I can give you something none of those store managers can give you. I can give you my experience and know-how so you'll learn to be a better salesperson faster. And I can give you a future opportunity, if you do a good job, to work into management and maybe someday even own a piece of the business. And, Rich, even if you want to go to work with a chain store later, you'll learn things here that will put you ahead of the pack climbing the career ladder there.

"So, Rich, it's up to you. You have to decide what kind of person you are, what you want for your future, and how much you value what I can teach you. If you do your job well, I can assure you you'll make a top income for our industry and probably much more than in a shopping center. But I can pay you a high income only if you help build a big business from the solid base I start you with."

If you were Rich, would you want to work for Arnold or a chain store manager?

BALONEYISM #7

*A Low Price Is the Most
Important Thing
And the Opposite Baloneyism:
Price Isn't Important When It Comes to
Color and Design*

Both statements are wrong, and both statements are right. Dozens of textbooks have been written on pricing policy, but it's easy to get confused with conflicting principles. When should a price be low? When should it be high? It's one of the most important decisions for the Bootstrap Entrepreneur in the new business. The key lies in customer-perceived values and how you establish your competitive edge.

If you sell a branded product that is the same quality wherever it is bought, you can be assured price is critical. On the other hand, if it is a fashion item where color, design, and artistic value are significant, you can be assured price is not so critical but *within a category*.

For example, many women will pay $180 for a dress in the color and fashion they want instead of paying $125 for equal tailoring but unsatisfactory design. Still, that does not mean they will pay $400, which is a whole different price category. Always remember you're dealing in price categories.

Barbara's Baby Furniture

Barbara operated a charming baby furniture store in a strip shopping center near a major mall. She had been in business three years. Although she had good customer traffic and sold a lot of furniture, she wasn't making the money she deserved. Income covered operating expenses, but Barbara barely earned minimum wage, considering the long hours she put in.

When Barbara started out, furniture sales reps cautioned her she would be up against big competitors. They recommended low pricing to compete. Barbara took the advice, but lately, she had been wondering if low prices were part of her profit problem. Barbara knew her customers liked her and the store. She always had creative ideas for displays and room layouts. She used color beautifully. Customers would even offer to pay Barbara to come to their homes to get ideas on how to decorate a child's room.

Barbara Could Do What Big Stores Couldn't

One day Barbara got sick and tired of making so little profit. She decided to raise her prices, even at the risk of ruining her business. Overnight she repriced everything in the store 10 percent higher. She decided that if all the customers quit buying, she could make more money working for someone else. But Barbara was wise. At the same time she raised prices, she added new, more decorative displays. Then she put up a sign offering to make a free home visit for customers needing several items of furniture for a child's room.

To Barbara's surprise, instead of fewer customers, even more customers came in. They appreciated Barbara's ideas and her personality. They just couldn't get those benefits at big stores.

The result? Barbara made $25,000 a year more immediately just by raising prices. The entire price increase was all net profit because there was no increase in advertising or overhead costs. Even better, her reputation for creative personal service continued to grow, and more and more customers sought out her store. Truly, Barbara learned that low price is not the most important thing.

Gloria's Art Gallery

Gloria loved to visit art galleries, and she had an exquisite collection of contemporary sculpture. She was bored and wanted to express her independence. *Why not open an art gallery?* she thought. She knew some exceptional nearby artists and was familiar with the market and trade shows. Many of Gloria's friends appreciated good art, and somehow it just seemed like the gallery would work well.

Gloria knew she needed a consistent design theme and decided on contemporary sculpture, paintings, and art objects. Her friends were paying from $2,000 to $3,500 for many items, and up to $10,000 for exceptions. Gloria felt if an item had an appealing design, the public would pay a premium to get what they wanted.

Where Are the Customers?

Gloria had a gala opening and did a terrific job with promotion. Traffic through the store was solid. Everyone looked, but only a few bought. Gloria needed two sales a week to cover costs, but many weeks she had only one. Within six months reality set in. She thought about giving up, but she wasn't a quitter. She had been talking to a lot of lookers who came through the gallery. They seemed affluent but a little less so than her friends. They were also a little younger. The customers seemed to appreciate the quality and design Gloria offered, but the prices were a stretch.

Failure Brought Success

The ideal, Gloria decided, would be to go above standard decorative art found in furniture stores and shopping centers, which often sold for $70 to $300, yet stay below her current prices. After running a 50 to 70 percent off closeout sale to clear the old inventory, Gloria scoured the market and worked with her artist friends to find smart, unique designs in the $400 to $800 range. She also got a few exceptional pieces at $1,500. She had to make two sales a day, instead of two a week, to break even, but with her experience talking to lookers, she believed she could do it.

The new format was an instant success, reaching break-even in sixty days and building steadily from there. Gloria began enjoying her role: an art buyer for young professionals; and a supporter of emerging artists whose lesser known works were not yet priced at a premium. It was a great learning experience for Gloria. Yes, the public will pay more for good fashion and design but within a range they can afford.

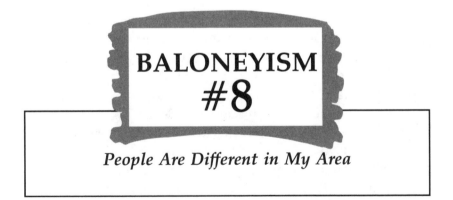

BALONEYISM
#8

People Are Different in My Area

Yes, people are different in your area and in every area. But they are also the same. Every area has sports fans and ballet lovers. Every area has home-proud and homeless. Whenever individuals say, "People in my area are different," they're telling about themselves, not about their city. They're really saying their minds are closed to learning why something does work or why their technique needs polish. Such people give up too quickly, have weak desire, or are just plain lazy. The Bootstrap Entrepreneur never uses "people are different in my area" as an excuse.

David and Mike Go to Market

David and Mike each owned a carpet store in a medium-size Ohio factory workers' town. Both went to the January carpet market in Atlanta. In addition to viewing all the new lines, they attended one of several industry seminars. The seminar leader was Tony, a vice president of sales at a national mill. His topic was "Better Your Profits with Better Carpet."

The theme of Tony's two-hour program was that relying on low-price builder's quality carpet, along with inventory of bolts and remnants to promote business, was a high-cost, low-profit way to run a carpet store. A better way, suggested Tony, was to sell color, fashion, and high quality at higher prices.

Mike interrupted Tony several times, saying, "Tony, people are different in my area. They're factory workers, some out of work, some retired. They just don't have the money to buy $20-a-yard carpet." And later Mike interrupted again, "Tony, people in my area move around every few years. They won't spend more money on something they won't keep long." And even later, he said, "Tony, builders in my area give only a $10 allowance for floor covering. I could never get people to pay twice as much."

Meanwhile, David was listening quietly and carefully. He didn't say much, but he learned a lot. Even though David was from the same town as Mike, he knew not all the people were the way Mike described them. Sure, there were price-conscious customers, and yes, they were a majority. But David had years ago decided to sell to the minority—the upper 30 percent income level in town. He focused on the better builders, and he showed their new home buyers how to get the best value. He explained how their beautiful $200,000 home could be enhanced substantially by investing an extra $2,000 to upgrade the standard-grade carpet to a premium quality the family would enjoy for years. And usually, it could be financed with the thirty-year mortgage loan for only pennies a day.

Mike had a three-thousand-square-foot store with lots of inventory and bolt ends. He constantly advertised low prices and low overhead, and the store looked the part. David had a small studio and was in it only a little while each day. He spent his time in the field calling on builders, Realtors, and others who could lead him to customers.

David's business sold only about one-third the yardage that Mike's business sold, but since David's prices were twice as high and his rent and advertising costs were less than half as much as Mike's, David actually made more profit at the end of the year. He dealt with quality customers he was proud to consider as friends, and he enjoyed more time with his family as well.

Yes, people were different in David and Mike's area, just as they are different in every area. But Mike's closed mind was the reason his business was failing, not because he lived in a small town in Ohio instead of Atlanta.

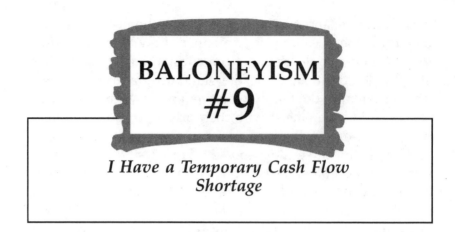

BALONEYISM #9

I Have a Temporary Cash Flow Shortage

The usual reason cash flow shortages are temporary is that the business is on the way out of business. Since it won't be around permanently, the shortage is only temporary.

If you're selling to a business that gives you this baloney, watch out!

You Can't Tell a Book by Its Cover

Jack's Food Store had been in the same location for fifteen years, a neighborhood starting to show age as young people grew up and moved away. Competition from two larger, more modern stores less than four miles away had been taking the edge off volume in recent years, but Jack's appeared ready to stay around forever.

It was just after Thanksgiving. Darren and Samuel, brothers ages sixteen and nineteen, had helped their dad harvest two truckloads of Christmas trees on farm property one hundred miles north of the Minnesota community where Jack's Food Store was located. For two days they had been calling on supermarkets to sell their trees direct for cash when they happened on Jack's Food Store. Jack needed trees. His selection wasn't enough to get through the season.

The boys were excited when they discovered Jack's need and his interest. He said he would give them a $1,000 order, the biggest they had received so far. With the sale under their belt, they would soon be finished and could return to their warm, cozy home. Everything seemed perfect.

Then as they were closing the sale and asked for the money, Jack said, "There's only one thing. I have a big warehouse delivery tomorrow, and I have a *temporary cash flow shortage.* How about if I give you boys $200 now, and you can pick up the balance on Monday after my big weekend traffic?"

The boys and their dad weren't sure what to do. They talked it over privately for some time. Finally, they decided to go along with Jack. He seemed like such a nice man, and his store had been around for years. Surely, he would keep his word, and they could wait until Monday for their $800.

Can you predict the outcome? Smiling Jack didn't have the money on Monday either. He gave them a few dollars more and stalled for another week and another and another. It was long after Christmas before they got even $200 additional. Months later, the boys gave up trying to collect, even though Jack still owed them $400.

Now, let's look at it from Jack's view. After all, why *should* Jack pay? Darren and Samuel weren't regular suppliers. Jack didn't need them again, and he knew the amount was too small for the boys to get a lawyer. Jack assuaged his guilt by saying to himself, *I'll pay them someday when I get the money.* Unfortunately, Jack never got the money, and "someday" never arrived.

The fact is, temporary cash flow shortages all too often become permanent. That's why as a new Bootstrap Entrepreneur, you never want to extend more credit to anyone than you're willing to give as a gift.

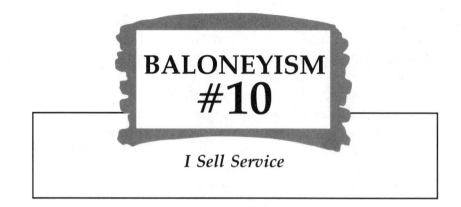

BALONEYISM #10

I Sell Service

What a nothing statement! If service is your strategy to beat competition, be explicit. Don't tell people you "sell service." Tell them *what* you do.

Do you have well-trained, attentive clerks to help customers with selections? Do you go to the customer's home? Do you offer expert advice on landscaping, household maintenance, or carpeting? Do you install your products promptly so customers don't waste time waiting? Think about what you do extra for your customers. Write it down so you and your employees understand it exactly. Then tell customers about the services you provide, not simply that you provide service.

What Service Could a Plumber Offer?

Let's say you have a plumbing business you target to homeowners who have an unexpected need or who want to do remodeling or replace old lines. Your yellow pages ad shouts "Best Service in Town." *But what does that mean?*

Do you have the friendliest telephone answerers? Is an expert plumber on call within fifteen minutes to talk on the phone? Can a qualified plumber be there in an hour if it's a serious emergency? Are you available after hours and on weekends? Do you guarantee satisfaction with rates and work? Do you carry most parts and replacements in the truck for one-call prompt repairs? Is your truck clean, new looking, and free from dents? Are your name and logo proudly and attractively painted on it so customers are pleased to have neighbors see the truck in their driveway?

Do you promptly return if there is any problem with the work you performed, and you do so pleasantly and without charge? Is your plumber uniformed, smiling, and friendly? Does he clean up when he's finished? Do you give each customer a confidential rating card to get feedback on your service? Do you follow up with thank-you notes?

If you do these things in the way of giving good service, tell people what you do. Put it in your ads and in a brochure. Be sure every plumber tells every customer. Never just say, "We give good service." Make the word *service* live with meaning and understanding.

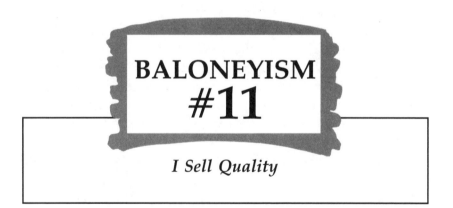

BALONEYISM #11

I Sell Quality

Selling quality is the same challenge as selling service. If you sell superior quality, say exactly what the difference is. Are the lapels on your suits sewn by hand so they lie flat and look like $1 million? Are your shoes styled only by top designers? Are they manufactured to exacting standards on a form-fitting last?

Whatever your edge in quality is, write it down. Communicate quality features precisely and in terms of *benefits to your customers.*

For example, "This luggage is the finest quality because it is made from durable parachute nylon. That means it will look better longer and give you years more service. The result is that it actually costs you less per year while you enjoy the pride of owning the best."

Get the word *quality* out of your vocabulary, except when you use it with other words to clearly communicate what it means.

Gilbert's Furniture Store

Jim Gilbert operated a furniture store specializing in upholstered sofas and chairs in a bedroom community about thirty miles north of a major Indiana city. Although the store sold some name brands, Gilbert's best line was from a regional manufacturer that made an exceptional product with low-cost local labor.

Business had long been successful for Gilbert's. It was started by Jim's dad in the 1950s. In fact, many customers traveled from the nearby city to take advantage of Gilbert's excellent quality and values. Then about two years ago, a large sofa specialty store opened in the primary market. With a huge advertising budget, a large selection, and low prices, Badger's began taking business from Jim Gilbert.

Jim knew his product was superior: kiln dried wood; eight-way hand-tied coil springs; the best foam cushions with a polyester wrap; and even goose down cushions for those who would pay a bit more. But his customers began to question Jim about why his prices were $100 to $200 more than those at Badger's. Badger's bragged about its quality, too, and it was hard to tell the difference just by sitting on each piece.

Jim thought about what to do. He realized it was his job to demonstrate superior quality in terms customers could believe in. But how to do it? Then the light switched on. He drove over to Badger's and bought one of their standard sofas off the floor for $1,100, then he trucked it back to his store. With a power saw Jim sliced the sofa in half. Then he did the same thing with one of his sofas.

Jim put both cutaway sofas in the front window. He had the Badger's register receipt enlarged to poster size. Although he disguised the name, the price was clearly visible, and customers who shopped both stores could guess where the receipt and sofa came from. In the cutaway models, customers could see the difference for themselves, the hand-tied coil springs compared to the squiggly noncoil springs Badger's used. They could see a difference in the cushion, both in the foam pad and in the polyester wrapping—there wasn't any wrapping in Badger's cushion.

That wasn't enough. Jim took the remaining half of each sofa and pulled it into pieces. He bought a giant balance scale and put it up front with one cushion on each side. The greater density of Jim's foam and the poly wrap weighed in much heavier and tipped the balance visibly lower.

Then he removed pieces of wood from each sofa and placed them in a vise on his work bench. One side was kiln dried wood from Jim's sofa, and the other was the green wood from Badger's sofa. Jim asked two employees to help demonstrate the difference in the wood. He handed each employee a blowtorch with a searing red-orange flame. And he switched on his video camera. With a big clock and sweep second hand in the background, each employee touched the flame to the wood. In less than two minutes the kiln dried wood burned; the green wood smoked and charred. After they removed the blow torches, the dry wood kept burning, and the other wood smoldered.

Next Jim had large signs made: DENSE FOAM—MORE COMFORTABLE—HOLDS UP FOR YEARS . . . KILN DRIED WOOD STAYS STURDY AND SOLID . . . HAND-TIED COILS WON'T CRUSH AND CAVE IN.

With the cutaway sofas, the large scale, the repeating video, and the signs, Jim clearly demonstrated the quality of his furniture so his customers could tell the difference. Not only did Gilbert's fend off a strong competitor, but sales climbed higher than ever in its forty-two years of business.

Jim understood you can't just tell people you have better quality. You have to talk about and demonstrate every component. Daddy would have been proud.

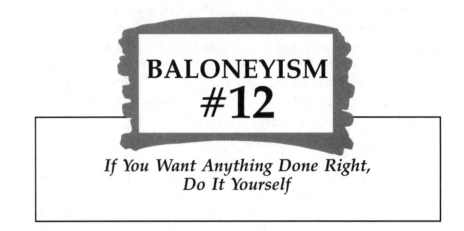

BALONEYISM #12

If You Want Anything Done Right, Do It Yourself

This statement is a surefire prescription to keep a small business small. It can be very smart to start small, but the Bootstrap Entrepreneur doesn't want to stay small long. Think of the wonderful qualities of employees and how you can help them get what they want as they help you get what you want.

California Detailin'

Evelyn might be called a shoe-shine person by some, but being an artistic leader in her profession and being located in California, she called herself a shoe detailer. When interviewed by the local daily paper, Evelyn said she detailed every pair of shoes personally to perfection. "I tried hiring employees a couple of times," she lamented, "but they just couldn't make shoes look as good as I can. I just don't want anyone else doin' shoes for my customers."

It's a classic case for small business owners. Many are perfectionists. They take so much pride in their work, and feel so needed and important doing it well, it gives them a sense of pride in being indispensable—just as Evelyn feels to this day. But are Evelyn's customers served best? What happens when Evelyn takes a vacation or is sick a few days or perhaps gets injured in an accident? And what happens to Evelyn's income then? Although it feels good to be indispensable, it may not serve the customers best who want service when they want it, and it may not serve the kids best when money is needed for rent and groceries.

What is the choice? A book could be written on this topic alone, but it all comes down to a couple of principles. First, allow people to make mistakes, to learn and grow. The business will survive. Second, explain why your high standards are so vital and invest time to train people so they can do high-quality work you are proud of.

Part 3

Why Be
a Bootstrap
Entrepreneur?

Chapter 7

What Kinds of People Are Entrepreneurs?

In the mid-1980s, William C. Dunkelberg, Ph.D., now dean of the business school at Temple University in Philadelphia, identified three significant varieties of business owners.

The Craftsperson   This person loves what she does and turns it into a business. This person could be an accountant, dentist, seamstress, plumber, Realtor, or any of dozens of different specialists and professionals who start a business. A lot of Bootstrap Entrepreneurs might fall into this category. The trap to watch out for, according to Dr. Dunkelberg, is that this person is so focused on the skill or specialty that she doesn't spend enough time learning business and marketing principles. She may have trouble building a high-profit enterprise.

The Pure Entrepreneur   This person wants to make a business bigger, better, and more profitable. He doesn't give a flip whether it's hamburgers or portable potties. Growth is the only goal. The classic entrepreneur is like a volcano erupting and violently punching through the ocean floor to create land mass where none existed before. Through eruptions, confusion, and stress, this type of entrepreneur creates a business where none existed before. If you're in the way, watch out. Stand clear from the fire until things cool off.

The Independence Seeker This person is so fiercely independent he can't work with anyone else. He knows all the answers. Everything has to be his way or not at all. This person usually starts a business because he can't hold a job. Of course, the business stays small because no competent person wants to work with somebody who knows all the answers. And no mentor will work with him because the Independence Seeker is limited to what he alone can do and he can seldom rise above mediocrity.

Chapter 8

Good Reasons to Be a Bootstrap Entrepreneur

You might want to become a Bootstrap Entrepreneur for lots of reasons. Let's look at some basic ones.

Control and Flexibility

Gaining control over your life, while doing something you believe in, is one sound reason to start a business of your own. Another is flexibility to work the hours you want. Of course, experienced entrepreneurs often say, "I have the freedom to work the hours I choose: eighty hours a week."

Fortunately if we do the right things, all the extra hours we put into the business will be doubly repaid down the road.

More important, to paraphrase Confucius:

. . . .

"Find a business you love, and you will never have to work another day in your life."

. . . .

When you have so much fun in your business that you can't tell your work from your play, why would you want to stop at 5:00 P.M.?

Government Policy

The United States government encourages small business formation. An entire department, the Small Business Administration (SBA), aids independent entrepreneurs in starting and succeeding in their own businesses. Although the SBA defines a small business as having up to five hundred employees, about 13 million businesses in America have fewer than five employees (over 80 percent of all businesses).

Tax Benefits

Your tax benefits as a Bootstrap Entrepreneur can be terrific. Your accountant can guide you best. Ask about operating your car or truck as a company vehicle (with proper signage and for proper purpose), acquiring office equipment, getting write-offs for space in your home used exclusively for business, and obtaining deductions for travel, business meals, entertainment, and other business needs, which may be combined with personal travel or entertainment.

A corporate paycheck might have to be 30 percent higher than your business income for you to enjoy the same after-tax standard of living.

Financial Cornerstone

For many Bootstrap Entrepreneurs, owning a business is the cornerstone to their financial plans. Your profit potential in the early years may be less than you want but don't overlook the potential to increase your net worth.

Net worth is what you *own* minus what you *owe*. Besides income, a well-managed business can build increased net worth every year. It's like putting money in a savings account.

For example, let's assume you invest $40,000 in a new business and you borrow the money to do it. Let's also assume you build the business so it has a good reputation, a solid customer base, and a healthy volume of sales. The business is now worth much more because of your efforts.

In the first five years if someone asked you how much money you took out every year, the answer might be so little as to be embarrassing. But look again at what you "saved."

If you paid off your original investment bank loan from business revenue, that's like $40,000 you saved—your net worth is now that much higher. Even better, a profitable business with a promising future could have a market value of $100,000. That's real "savings" in your account—an average of $20,000 per year!

How much would you have to earn as an employee to save $20,000 per year?

Now, let's go a step further. Suppose you choose to sell your business. You might take $20,000 down and $80,000 over a period of four years. By adding on a reasonable rate of interest, you are likely to receive more than $25,000 per year.

Take your choice! Quit working, and get by on $25,000 for a few years. That way you gain back all those extra hours you put into your business. Or if you prefer, start a new business, and do it all over again. Obviously, some businesses may not do as well as this example, and some may do much better.

Chapter 9

Good Reasons *Not* to Be a Bootstrap Entrepreneur

Just as there are many reasons to start your own business, there are some good ones not to. Here are a few examples.

A Brand-New Idea

Let's say you have a brilliant idea that's never been done before anywhere. Maybe it's setting up a store with an endless variety of buttons so home sewers can find every possible one they need. Or maybe you love chocolate, and you believe chocolate lovers will flock to a store specializing in pies, confections, and all manner of things chocolate. Whatever your idea is, if it's never been done before, don't be the first.

Instead of finding a business new to the world, find a business new to your area. Unless you're a research scientist, engineer, or computer wizard or you have rights to a scientific breakthrough, never, never, start a business based on a new idea. Find someone, somewhere, who has already done it. Then do it better, or do it in a different place.

Do a Favor for Your Spouse

Perhaps, as a favor, you want to provide your spouse a project. Over the years I have seen doctors, lawyers, executives, and other busy breadwinners who felt guilty because they weren't spending enough time with their spouses. The answer? Assuage guilt by buying a business.

It always fails. Why?

As an example, let's assume a husband buys a business for his wife. It's not the wife's motive to make the business succeed. It's not her idea. It's his. She is simply appeasing her husband one more time.

The point is, whoever is going to run the business should be a person who really wants it, a person who wants it enough to find a way to pay for it on her own.

Bored Silly

Perhaps you're bored. You want something to do, but you don't like the confines of working for someone else. Maybe the kids have grown up. Possibly, you just retired. However, unless there is no investment, unless you are doing it for fun, please do not start a business. Go into charity work instead. You will benefit yourself and the world far more.

Retiree's Nightmare

Don and Betty had been married thirty-five years. Their son and two daughters were grown, and Don and Betty were grandparents of four. A year ago, Don retired from his position as human resources executive for a major automaker and moved from Michigan to the snow-free climate in southwestern Florida. Betty grew up when mothers raised kids full-time. Other than participating in volunteer projects at school, homemaking was her only career. Don and Betty were not well off, but between Don's pension plan and

Betty's frugality over the years, they accumulated $130,000 in savings. With conservative investments and Social Security, they could live modestly, mortgage-free in an attractive manufactured home community.

After a year of the quiet life, Don was getting restless. At the same time, Betty began thinking it would be nice if they could afford a small camper and travel occasionally. At first, Don thought about getting a job, but opportunities were limited in Florida for men over sixty.

Why Not Open a Business?

After talking it over together, Don and Betty decided to explore the possibility of a small business of their own. They knew what they didn't want: long hours in a shopping center, a huge inventory, or high cost overhead. Yet, they were unsure about what they did want. They spent weeks scouring business opportunity advertising, franchise magazines, and library publications. Finally, they decided a small print shop might be the answer. They considered franchising but dismissed the idea. The monthly minimum fees seemed to require a larger business than Don and Betty wanted. Instead, they talked to an equipment supplier who assured them he could provide all the tips and ideas they needed to build a successful business.

Don figured that by eliminating the franchise fee of $20,000, the equipment itself would be a solid investment, and in a worst-case scenario, it could be liquidated without too much loss. The $45,000 investment seemed reasonable. With a down payment of 50 percent, the lease on the equipment was only about $500 per month.

Their idea was to hire a pressman so that Don wouldn't have to get ink under his fingernails and learn the complexities of production. He planned to spend time meeting customers and promoting the business. Betty would work the counter and pleasantly greet customers as they came in the door. Soon, they found a location with rent at $1,500 per month.

Things Get Going

Things seemed to be coming together pretty well, although making leasehold improvements and installing the equipment were bigger jobs than expected and cost an extra $3,600. Within a few weeks, it was time to hire employees, and thirty days later, they held their opening. In less than sixty days, Don and Betty began to wonder if they had done the right thing. By the end of four months as new business operators, they knew they had made a disastrous mistake.

Their first pressman quit in less than six weeks but not before emptying the cash register on his way out. The second one showed up drunk on two occasions, frightening Betty so much she didn't want to be in the shop unless Don was there. Being inside more cut down on his time promoting business. When Don did call on customers, he found things he didn't expect. He called on large and small businesses in the community, and yes, there was a lot of printing being done. But Don never realized how many print shop competitors were already fighting for business. Some competitors operated out of their basements and charged low prices Don couldn't match. Others had classy well-established shops with a well-known reputation. It was a lot tougher breaking into the market than Don thought it would be.

After the third time the pressman turned up drunk, and with overhead costs running $1,200 more each month than their revenues coming in, Don and Betty realized they couldn't afford to hire any more employees until their sales got higher. Don began running the presses in the afternoon and evening. It really wasn't his cup of tea. Sometimes he would have to run a job four or five times to get it right. The wasted paper and ink and the extra delays were torturous.

Struggle On

Nevertheless, Don and Betty decided to give it their best, hoping things would turn around as people got to know them. They longed for the leisure life of only six months ago. Now each day was booked from 8:00 A.M. to after 6:00 P.M. and at least a half day on Saturday. They struggled on for over a year. In the last three or four months, costs were being covered, but there wasn't enough to hire another person. They realized they would be chained to the business a long, long time. They just didn't want to live the rest of their retirement that way.

Time to Sell

Together, they decided to sell the business. Selling it as a going operation, they might recover the $22,500 paid down on the equipment but probably not the $18,000 they lost in start-up and overhead expenses. That's when they discovered used printing equipment was a glut on the market and rarely brought over 30 percent of the original value. Don and Betty soon recognized they would be lucky to walk away without paying more on the lease.

It took another four months of struggling, but finally, Don and Betty liquidated the business and escaped their torture chamber. They tallied up the final results: gone were a year and a half of hard work, and their bank account was $38,000 slimmer than when they started. Instead of adding to their income, Don and Betty would have to get by on a lower income or find some type of work as a supplement.

What Happened?

Why didn't it work? Lots of reasons, beginning with the lack of careful investigation about competition and actual value of equipment. And they lacked know-how in the business. Possibly, they could have worked in a shop to get experience first. But beyond that, Don and Betty's entire decision-making process was based on the wrong premise: *the idea of just dabbling at something, expecting a nice income, without really working at it.*

Is it possible for anyone to work at a business during retirement without being consumed by it? Yes, but even a part-time supplemental income business should be approached seriously because it is *still* a business!

There are some good reasons not to start your own business. You probably have a feel for which is the right answer for you. Just be sure it's not fear you feel. Everyone feels fear before starting a new venture, yet over 3 million entrepreneurs find the courage to do it every year. So can you.

Ten Principles
for Bootstrap Entrepreneurs

1. Keep your job awhile. Start the business part-time.
2. Avoid rent. Work from your home or a coffee shop.
3. Don't hire employees. Use consultants, contractors, and services.
4. Avoid inventory. Sell first; buy later.
5. Think customers first, last, and always. Know how to find them and keep them.
6. Don't sell on credit.
7. Know your purpose. Know your mission. Put it in writing now.
8. Dare to risk. Success requires it. If you fail, you will achieve greater success later.
9. Make a friend. Do it everywhere with everyone.
10. Dream big. Operate small.

Chapter 10

Will You
Make Money?

The answer is a definite maybe. Yes, there is vast potential. Bootstrap Entrepreneurs always plan to make money. Generally, they do. Sometimes they don't. Often the amount of income planned for is optimistic. And sometimes it takes longer to achieve. Does it matter? In a way, yes. In a way, no.

Ask the person who owns a business, "Do you feel you're working too hard for too little money?" The answer is always, "Yes!" Then ask, "Would you be better off working for someone else?" The answer will be, "Maybe." Then ask, "Do you have any plans to quit your business and go to work for someone else?" The answer will always be, "NO!"

Why this ambivalent attitude by entrepreneurs? Because there are many forms of compensation in life. Some are financial; some, emotional; and some, philosophical. Belief in the possibility of improving one's future is essential. Bottom line, entrepreneurs believe they have the potential to do better on their own. They won't sell out their future working for someone else.

Pet Store Perseverance

Alice and Kevin grew up on farms in a small western Nebraska town. Both loved animals. Their pets included two Siamese cats, a dachshund, a beagle, and a horse boarded in the country.

As Kevin turned thirty, he and Alice began thinking about their future. Their midwestern values held that you pretty much get out of life what you put into it. Kevin didn't have a college degree, and Alice was bumping against a glass ceiling. The one answer that seemed to make most sense for them to achieve their potential was to start a business of their own.

For more than a year, they attended franchise shows, subscribed to business opportunity publications, and did research at their local library. Their savings were about $10,000. Both sets of parents, though far from wealthy, were solid financially. Last Christmas, Alice and Kevin talked to their folks about opening a business. They received cautious, but positive support. Alice's folks agreed to lend them $15,000 on a long-term basis, and Kevin's parents agreed they would cosign a loan up to $20,000.

The result was a total capital base of $45,000. Not a lot, but their bills were paid except for one car payment.

Time to Act

In the spring of 1989, they got serious about finding a business. One Thursday, as Alice studied the special franchising section in the *Wall Street Journal*, she excitedly spotted a new offer: Puppy Love Pet Stores. The total investment was over $100,000 but could be financed with $35,000 cash. She could hardly wait to tell Kevin about her discovery. For three months, they carefully investigated the franchisor, other similar franchises, and the possibilities of starting a pet store on their own. They knew they loved animals but decided the complexities of supply and marketing justified the investment in a franchise. They liked the people at Puppy Love. They believed in their sincerity and their willingness to give support to make the first Denver operation a showcase success. Before Thanksgiving, they opened the first Puppy Love Pet Store in a suburban mall.

Opening Kickoff

Thanks to good traffic in the mall, the cute puppies attracted a lot of people to look around the store. Kevin and Alice soon became quite good at turning lookers into customers. They enjoyed a brisk Christmas business, exceeding their break-even point (the level where sales cover expenses). As expected, January and February were soft, but by spring, they could cover expenses again.

Struggle Continues

Throughout the summer and fall, it was a struggle. Profits continued skimpy; their income was just over half the amount they made before. Still, they enjoyed themselves immensely. There was much in the business they hadn't expected with supplier dealings and paperwork and financial reports and matters like that, but both felt they were learning, and they welcomed the challenge. The franchisor continued to do as promised, providing valuable help and guidance. At the same time, Alice and Kevin helped the franchisor sell four additional units in Denver, and by the holiday season, the stores were advertising together, achieving more awareness and acceptance for the Puppy Love concept.

By their second December, they were truly excited. Their reputation was building, they believed in the business, their financial value was growing, and they felt they were doing the right thing for the long term to build their net worth. They began making payments to Alice's parents, and they were starting to get close to the income they were making a year and a half before.

Recession Surprise

Then the unexpected happened—a major aerospace firm announced a layoff of thousands just before Christmas. Within weeks more companies announced layoffs. As the recession deepened, shopping center traffic dropped. When shoppers did come in, they bought mainly supplies. Discretionary money for a new puppy was scarce, especially with veterinary and food bills.

Sales continued to slide, even lower than their first year in business. Alice and Kevin were stressed and distressed. By summer, they were running out of money. They had to do something. Maybe getting away would give them perspective. They arranged for an owner of another Puppy Love franchise to watch their store for three days while they got away to a friend's cabin in the mountains.

Time to Think

It was a quiet time, a contemplative time. Alice and Kevin asked themselves, Should we throw in the towel? Are we silly to struggle on? Over the next day and a half, they thought about many things: the jobs they had before, and what it was like working for someone else. They thought about their skills and experience and their options for the future. They thought about what they liked to do, what they were good at, and where they wanted to be in years to come. Most of all, they asked themselves, Do we really believe this is a good business? Over the long haul, will there be consumer demand? What do we want for our future? Where do we want to be five years from now?

By the end of the second day, Kevin and Alice made one important decision: neither ever wanted to work for someone else again. They definitely wanted their own business, and they were determined to see it through. That evening, they decided, "If it is our choice to see it through, and it is, let's give the business all we've got. Let's see what we can do to make Puppy Love a success." With two key decisions behind them, they prayed together and retired early. They slept better than they had in many nights.

A New Day, a New Life

Refreshed, the next morning they began to brainstorm all the possibilities they could think of to make Puppy Love a success. They thought up dozens of ideas: featured pet of the month . . . in-store seminars on pet care . . . lectures by respected veterinarians . . . joint merchandising programs with obedience trainers and kennels . . . special mailings to past customers . . . a campaign to owners suggesting how much happier their single animal would be with a friend to play with . . . and on and on. By midafternoon, they developed over forty ideas to promote business. They winnowed them down to the ten best possibilities.

They decided their number one priority was to mail a flier to each customer who bought a pet or pet supplies during the past two years. Then they would telephone each one personally. They would check with customers to be sure they were satisfied with Puppy Love's service, and they would encourage them to purchase new supplies or a new animal or urge the customers to refer others to Puppy Love.

You Get What You Put In

Within ninety days, the results began to show. Other stores in the mall were still quiet, but there was always excitement at Puppy Love. The regional manager for the franchisor came often to see what they were doing so the franchisor and other stores could learn from Kevin and Alice's ideas.

By their third Christmas, even in the recession, sales were

at the highest level ever. In fact, their store was the number one Puppy Love franchise in the six-state Rocky Mountain area.

Finally with the Christmas rush behind, they paused to look at each other, to smile, and to count their blessings. They knew what they believed in, they knew what they wanted, and they discovered within themselves an inner resourcefulness they had never known before. Even though the business didn't make as much money as they expected in the first two years, they knew they had learned a valuable lesson worth many times more than the income lost from a job. Kevin and Alice learned they could stand on their own feet, take control of their lives, and build something for their future.

Is Money the Only Thing?

If money is the only thing driving you today, think long and hard about whether you're ready to be a Bootstrap Entrepreneur. You may not make as much money as you want as quickly as you want to make it. Yet, someday you may make much more owning a business than working for someone else. That's why the word *entrepreneur* means "one who assumes the risk of business." And that's why if you are to grow, to develop, to use your full potential, you must take risks. You can do it. Don't settle for leftover crumbs from the banquet table of life.

Are You Ready?

Supportive spouse?

- Works full-time for an employer
- Plans to work in business

Sense of urgency?

- What action have you taken so far?
- What action do you plan soon?

Why do you want your own business?

- Avoid boredom
- Want to change careers
- Have a long-term plan

Pleasing personality?

- Positive attitude
- Willingness to serve others
- Emotional stability

Good health?

- Eat right
- Exercise often
- Become ill rarely
- Possess energy and stamina

Chapter 11

Are You Ready?

Should you consider becoming a Bootstrap Entrepreneur? Test yourself.

Instructions: Mark an X in the column that most closely represents your situation.

	1	2	3	Score
1. Are you married?	No	Yes; children at home	Yes; no children at home	
2. When do you want to start?	Uncertain	6–18 mos.	0–6 mos.	

3. Have you ever attended a business opportunity show?	No	Yes, alone	Yes, with spouse or partner
	_____	_____	_____	_____
4. Have you ever requested information on a franchise or business?	No	Once	2 or more
	_____	_____	_____	_____
5. Why do you want your own business?	Need something to do	Don't like job	Control life and future
	_____	_____	_____	_____
6. What is your physical health and wellness (sick days in last 12 months)?	3 +	1–3	0
	_____	_____	_____	_____

7. What is your spouse's interest and involvement in the business? (If spouse is or will be involved full-time, do not check any column.)

Little interest	Supportive, not involved	Involved part-time	
_____	_____	_____	_____

8. Have you ever been in an independent business of your own?

3+ times	Never	1–2 times	
_____	_____	_____	_____

9. Do you have any sales experience?

None	Some	Extensive	
_____	_____	_____	_____

Personality Characteristics	Little	Moderate	High	
10. Are you enthusiastic?	_____	_____	_____	____
11. Are you responsible on follow-up?	_____	_____	_____	____
12. Do you like to work with people?	_____	_____	_____	____
13. Do you enjoy serving people?	_____	_____	_____	____
14. Do you read books and listen to tapes?	Under 6 per year	6–12 per year	12+ per year	
	_____	_____	_____	____
15. Do you get depressed or discouraged?	Time to time	Seldom	Very rare	
	_____	_____	_____	____

16. What is your debt (not counting home and car, our family is in debt by more than our savings)?

A lot	Some	None	
_____	_____	_____	____

17. What are your income sources?

None—unemployed	You are employed	Self and spouse employed	
_____	_____	_____	____

18. If your spouse works, but you have no income from your business for 6 months, how would the family maintain its living standard?

Go into debt	Use savings	Live on spouse's income	
_____	_____	_____	____

19. What is the amount of your available home equity (market value less mortgage)?

$0–$9,999	$10,000–$30,000	$30,000+	
_____	_____	_____	____

20. Did your parents or your spouse's parents own a business?	Neither self nor spouse	Either self or spouse	Both self and spouse	
	_____	_____	_____	_____

Total _____

Scoring Yourself

Basic scoring: Award yourself one point for each answer in column 1, two points for each answer in column 2, and three points for each answer in column 3.

Bonus scoring for questions 16 through 20: Double the points for any answers in column 2 or column 3.

Scoring Guidelines (Maximum 75 Points)

60–75 You have exceptionally strong entrepreneurial qualifications. You may already be in a business of your own or should be soon.

45–59 You are in a range with many Bootstrap Entrepreneurs. Consider starting a business. Continue to work on areas that need improvement.

30–44 You are in a marginal range. Take time to prepare until weak areas are improved (possibly one to two years).

Under 30 Starting the move to own a business is not wise now. If you really want to be a Bootstrap Entrepreneur, remedy areas that need work. It may be within your grasp. Set a plan to develop yourself, probably in sales and people skills.

Understanding Why These Questions Affect Your Future As a Bootstrap Entrepreneur

1. *Are you married?* Marriage is a great asset to business success. With no children, a spouse has even more time available for the business. Ideally, your spouse should continue the present career to provide income while also working in the business part-time.

2. *When do you want to start?* An "uncertain" response indicates dreams more than plans. Wanting to be in business within six months indicates a firm decision. Good luck!

3. *Have you ever attended a business opportunity show?* You may find nothing of interest in business opportunity and franchise shows. Nevertheless, if you are seriously thinking about your own business, explore every possibility. Leave no stone unturned.

4. *Have you ever requested information on a franchise or business?* The same comment applies as in question 3.

5. *Why do you want your own business?* If you want something to do, go into charity work. If you don't like your job, that's a good reason to think about a business of your own but don't hop out of the frying pan into the fire. Search yourself. Are you really ready to take control of your life and take the risk of a better future? You should be making a positive move in a direction you want to go, not simply escaping from an intolerable job.

6. *What is your physical health and wellness?* You must be healthy to own and operate a business. You can't afford to get sick. If you lost more than one day to illness in the last year, watch out.

7. *What is your spouse's interest and involvement in the business?* As noted in question 1, the ideal is for your spouse to be involved on a part-time basis

while continuing a career. Next most valuable is for your spouse to be supportive but not involved. Last, if your spouse has little interest in the business, *beware*. This is a definite sign you have not worked out common goals within your marriage. Your new business could contribute to marital difficulties.

8.   *Have you ever been in an independent business of your own?* The ideal is to have succeeded in a business, gaining good insights and experience. If you have never been in business, you are in the same boat with a lot of folks and will have the same things to learn. If you've been in three or more businesses, the assumption is, they were not successful. What's going to make it different this time?

9.   *Do you have any sales experience?* This area is fundamental. Every Bootstrap Entrepreneur is constantly selling and promoting the business. However, a person with a friendly, outgoing personality has more assets than a grump with a lot of sales experience. If you like people and are willing to go the extra mile, dozens of books and cassette tape programs will help you polish your sales skills.

10.–13. *Are you enthusiastic? Are you responsible on follow-up? Do you like to work with people? Do you enjoy serving people?* The appropriate answers should be self-evident. If you do not understand the point of these questions, exercise extreme caution about going into your own business.

14.   *Do you read books and listen to tapes?* Research and personal experience indicate that successful Bootstrap Entrepreneurs constantly develop personality and business skills. Reading one book a month is only for openers. Every Bootstrap Entrepreneur should be listening to an audiotape or reading a book on a weekly basis. As self-image develops, so will the success of the business.

15. *Do you get depressed or discouraged?* Everyone gets discouraged from time to time. What counts is the way you deal with it. If you curl up and withdraw for more than a day or so, be extra cautious about getting into a business of your own. Every business is fraught with problems and setbacks. They go with the territory.

16. *What is your debt?* Ideally, have some savings in the bank, say one-third of your initial investment in the business. That does not mean you will use your savings. You may choose to borrow the entire amount. But having savings tells much more about your common sense and reliability. If you do not have savings, I hope you're not in debt with credit cards and department store accounts. If you have a credit problem, clear it up before you consider your own business. It's one thing to start at zero; it's something else to start in a hole.

17. *What are your income sources?* The point of this question concerns financial stability. Actually, whether you and your spouse are employed is secondary, but in most families one person, if not both, should be employed to stabilize family income before starting a new business.

18. *If your spouse works, but you have no income from your business for 6 months, how would the family maintain its living standard?* Obviously, the best news is being able to survive on your spouse's income only. Next best is getting by with your spouse's income plus savings. Having to go in debt to survive month to month is scary. Consider cutting back your standard of living or making other adjustments to avoid debt at all costs.

19. *What is the amount of your available home equity?* Home equity is the cornerstone to finance most new businesses. Having $30,000 to $100,000 available to draw down on a revolving line of credit is one of the

best ways to do it. Anything less than $10,000 is of marginal value. But if you are determined and confident and willing to start on a shoestring, you may need every penny.

20. *Did your parents or your spouse's parents own a business?* One of the most favorable signs for successful Bootstrap Entrepreneurs is to have parents who owned a business. You learned more from osmosis than you realize: what it takes to satisfy customers; normal anxiety when business is slow; importance of financial statements; money management; and other things. About 50 percent of new business owners have a parent who owned a business.

Yes, it takes favorable conditions and good attitudes to last in your new business. If some of your conditions or attitudes need work, start working on them today. And remember, this test is not a final answer. That's why you're reading this book—so read on. When it feels right, you'll know it. Then go for it!

Chapter 12

Preparing
Yourself

So, how do you prepare to become a Bootstrap Entrepreneur? When should you start? What school courses should you take? What books should you read? What tape programs should you listen to? All are good questions. Whether you want to start your new business one month or five years from now, the time to prepare is today.

You might think the first step is to take business courses at school. Well, school courses aren't going to hurt a Bootstrap Entrepreneur, but they may not help much for the business you want.

Business school courses tend to be on economics, employee management, law, and other issues. You will get lots of information on accounting, labor relations, marketing channels of distribution, and other things.

But the Bootstrap Entrepreneur really needs to know only two things: (1) how to find customers, and (2) how to spend less money than you take in. Of the two, how to find customers is the more important.

Since finding customers is more important for your new

business, it stands to reason a Bootstrap Entrepreneur should focus on sales skills, merchandising, promotion, and customer relations. Yes, that may seem like a strange way to begin. Perhaps you're saying, "Look, I'm an accountant, and I want to learn to be a better accountant before I start my business." Or you may be saying, "I want to learn more about _____" (fill in gardening, advertising, architecture, plumbing, or whatever else may be the specialty of your expected business).

The fact is, you probably already know quite a lot about what you plan to do. Chances are, you've been doing it already. But you may not have been promoting new customers. That may be a whole new skill for you.

A great beginning for an aspiring Bootstrap Entrepreneur is to read books and listen to tapes about personal improvement, goal setting, and sales. Fortunately, it's easy to do. There are low-cost books and tapes at every bookstore. Or get them free at the library. Every Bootstrap Entrepreneur should be on a personal improvement program before and after starting a new business. Dale Carnegie's fabulous book *How to Win Friends and Influence People* is the starting point. Read it once now, and reread it at least once every year.

Also start watching advertising and promotion ideas used by competitors. Look for ads that are repeated. They are probably used a second time because they worked the first time.

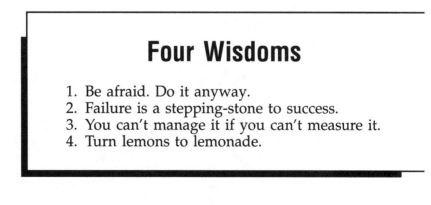

Four Wisdoms

1. Be afraid. Do it anyway.
2. Failure is a stepping-stone to success.
3. You can't manage it if you can't measure it.
4. Turn lemons to lemonade.

Chapter 13

How to Think Like a Bootstrap Entrepreneur

Anyone who studies personal improvement already knows that *attitude is more important than reality*. It is what you believe that counts. Belief in yourself, belief in your business, and belief in your customers will affect the success of your business. Belief, or faith, is the most significant of all attitudes for the Bootstrap Entrepreneur. If you develop faith, everything else will follow.

The way you think and what you think about will determine whether you start, and whether you succeed, in your new business. Thoughts are the beginning point of every worthwhile project in life. Whether building a skyscraper or putting a woman on Mars is the goal, it begins with a thought in the mind of a human being. Volumes have been written about attitudes. But here are some essential nuggets for Bootstrap Entrepreneurs:

Have a positive attitude Strangely enough, most people think they have a positive attitude, even if they are negative. Cultivating a positive attitude is perhaps the single most important lifelong endeavor for any Bootstrap Entrepreneur. It's difficult because it means keeping a positive expectancy while planning rationally to reduce risk of an unpleasant reality.

Be open-minded If you respect someone, try to see why the person's idea might work rather than why it might not. Being open-minded is vital if you want to be coached to success.

Be willing to listen This quality is essential for open-mindedness.

Be willing to serve As a Bootstrap Entrepreneur, you are a person starting a business with minimum financial capital. But there is another kind of capital—human capital. You have your entire life to render in service for the purpose of achieving your goals. How wonderful it is that a Bootstrap Entrepreneur with little financial capital has an abundance of human capital! Use it to build a successful business.

What about people who do not have these attitudes? How does the difference affect the business? Try interviewing a dozen or so independent business owners. You'll start to see a pattern distinguishing the winners from the losers. We so often hear about good attitudes, sometimes it's easier to recognize good attitudes by contrasting them with wrong ones. Here are a couple of the wrong attitudes you may recognize.

Chicago Manager

One manager of independent dealers in the Chicago area told this story: "In my territory a handful of business owners do a great job and have a nice business. The people in another group are pretty well achieving their goals, and while not top performers, they are happy with their businesses. Then I have another group, probably about one-third, I classify as PIMAS and YABBOTS.

"These dealers are often at the bottom in sales, and they are always complaining. PIMA means 'people in my area' (are different), and YABBOT means when they hear a solution to a problem, they respond, 'Yeah, but . . .' I've come to realize these people find fault with everything and everyone, except themselves. In their minds, the customers in their area are ungrateful cheapskates. Their suppliers pick on them and foul up their orders more than those of other dealers. They also feel there are too many competitors and other things. These dealers look for reasons why a solution won't work rather than why it will. They make excuses for themselves instead of finding what they can personally do to take control. I think they enjoy playing victim rather than taking responsibility.''

California Distributor

Another example is a distributor for a nationally respected food supplement network marketing company. Her spouse was the breadwinner, and her distributorship was intended to provide supplemental income to put the kids through college. Her business was not doing well, and she considered it to be the fault of her company. She also felt that other distributors in the same organization were taking away her customers. She took frequent trips out of town, she was often unavailable to her customers, and she rarely attended the many sales meetings provided by her upline master distributor. The meetings were to train her how to find and keep customers.

Nevertheless, she believed her low production was someone else's fault. She went on a rampage writing letters to corporate executives, to her upline, and to other distributors, spending hours and hours of her own time and of others' time. Her managers and fellow distributors attempted to respond respectfully but soon became frustrated and unable to deal with her unbusinesslike attitudes. But since she was a person who had no other job, and whose spouse supported her, she had lots of time to write letters and create trouble for others who needed to make a living.

The distributor was never able to realize that her customers went to other distributors because they weren't getting the attention they deserved and needed. The distributor has not learned to this day that just because she meets a potential customer or even makes a sale to someone, she does not have the right to a customer's business forever. Customers require care and feeding like a puppy. Customers have the God-given right to buy their products wherever, whenever, and from whomever they please.

Corny Qualities Count

Positive, upbeat, open-minded attitudes are necessary for a Bootstrap Entrepreneur. Each of us is responsible for personal success. These "Be Happy Attitudes," as the Reverend Robert Schuller calls them, may seem corny, but having guided hundreds of Bootstrap Entrepreneurs, I remember no one with these qualities who failed, and no one without them who succeeded beyond mediocrity. This chapter can help you start today on your attitude development program, then expand your personal growth with the excellent books suggested in the Bibliography.

Chapter 14

Gender
Differences

More and more women in America and the world are becoming Bootstrap Entrepreneurs. Women bring a special difference to business. Ignoring these differences would be folly.

Studies have shown women to be more process oriented while men are more results oriented. Women are more likely than men to follow policies well, to play by the rules. They are more likely than men to build a consensus, to find a win-win solution for all. Men are more hunter-killer competitors.

Women are taught from early childhood to avoid risk and danger. Men are taught from early childhood to be courageous to face danger. For example, a boy may break an arm falling from a tree. He may scrape his knee trying to be the fastest on roller skates. Traditional folkways have discouraged this behavior in women, so women must work hard to overcome aversion to risk.

Does that mean the female Bootstrap Entrepreneur is less likely to succeed than her male counterpart? No. Women survive in business at virtually the same rate as men. As mothers, wives, caretakers, and caregivers, women often operate service businesses with fewer employees, and many are home based.

However, regardless of whether the size of the business is large or small, and whether the income is high or low, attitudes of women about business are strikingly similar. The *Wall Street Journal* reported a survey about attitudes of women executives earning $100,000 to $150,000 per year. Although one might expect high-income women to be more results oriented and individually competitive, just the opposite was true. The women took pride in building consensus, in associating with quality, and in maintaining high ethical standards. Effective business results were a by-product of doing the right things rather than being an end in themselves.

Things to Consider

My wife, Valerie, has worked with dozens of new women business owners. Asked what a woman should consider when thinking about a business of her own, Valerie shared these thoughts:

1. If family is a consideration, write down the hours you need for your family as a given. Then the business should work around the remaining hours.
2. Love what you do. Most women are successful when they do things they enjoy and believe in. If you like art, consider retailing art or operating a frame shop, for example.
3. Bring pleasure to others. Most women like to see people enjoy things they sell. Yes, receiving the money gives self-esteem and sense of worth, but money alone is not enough. The satisfaction of the user is important to women.
4. Organizing is easy. Most women are good at making lists, planning time, and juggling different people's

needs. Women also usually excel at following through and keeping commitments. Find a business that values these qualities. It will give you an edge.

5. Women usually enjoy and want to identify with high quality. They identify personally with the product as a reflection of who they are. There may be good money operating an auto salvage business, but probably few women will want to do it.

6. Women commonly are more patient than men. Three different veterinarians told Valerie to have our poodle groomed by a woman. Dog grooming is more than just a business to women. They take time and feel pride in a quality result.

Businesses That Suit Women

Women often shine in grass-roots businesses, as Valerie calls them. Think of these women who started in a small way and became a huge success.

Jean Nidetch started a weight reduction support group in her basement. Before long, Weight Watchers was a national success story.

Judi Shepphard Missett got a few neighbors to do aerobics together in her home. She added music and simple dance steps, and an industry was born with Jazzercize leading the way.

Joan Barnes got kids to have fun and stay healthy at the same time as she got them to exercise in her family room. Eventually, Gymboree became a three-hundred-unit international franchisor.

Debbie Fields baked the best cookies in the neighborhood. Today, many people believe Mrs. Fields's cookies are the best in the world.

Sue Bowers in Indianapolis won prizes at the county fair for the best decorated cakes before starting her own successful catering business.

List Your Talents

Women often take their talents and experience for granted. Don't. List things you like to do: bake, cook, sew, type, teach, manage, entertain, sell, write, play a piano, love kids, care for older people, shop, tidy up, paint, drive, dress up, socialize, exercise, or play tennis, cards, or golf. Whatever it is, there may be a seed of a great business inside your brain. Pull it out.

If you live in the city, bring the city some country—country cookin', bakin', quilts, crafts, or whatever. If you live in the country, bring the country some city fashion jewelry, fine clothing, art, gourmet food, interior design, or other things people would love to have but don't want to drive miles to get.

Women have special talents, and many women have excellent, classic examples of a Bootstrap Entrepreneur business. More and more women are growing more and more successful in business every day. Why shouldn't you be one of them?

Helpful Organizations

The following organizations specialize in providing women entrepreneurs assistance in starting and operating a business. Be sure to contact them before you quit your job and open your business. You won't have time later.

- Small Business Administration (SBA)
  Office of Women's Business Ownership (OWBO)
  202-205-6673
- Minority Business Development Centers
  202-377-1936
- Support groups
  National Association of Women Business Owners
  312-922-0465

National Association for Female Executives
212-645-0770

- Local economic development offices
- Chambers of commerce
- Continuing education programs
- State offices

Chapter 15

Husbands and Wives

Should couples consider Bootstrap Entrepreneuring? What are the pluses and minuses of husbands and wives working together? I have worked with my wife, Valerie, as a business partner for most of our twenty-nine married years. I have also helped scores of couples operate their business together. I've gained some insights based on this experience.

If your marriage is rocky, partnering in business will accelerate its demise. At the opposite, if you have a sound marriage, working together may bring things to the surface that, once confronted, improve and enhance your marriage beyond words.

Marriage, like business and life itself, is never perfect. All three are ongoing struggles. There are victorious times, and there are dark times. No Bootstrap Entrepreneur should expect more of a business or of marriage than any of us should expect of life itself.

If you and your spouse are considering a business together, talk it through as completely as you can. Be really honest with each other. Ask what each of you wants from the business, from the marriage, and from life itself. Here are some pros and cons to stimulate your discussion.

Pros

- You have common goals and common reasons to achieve them.
- Because you understand each other, you will communicate almost intuitively. No employee would understand you the same way.
- Because both of you are owners, you will be more attentive to customers and more responsible following up problems.
- Each of you brings a unique perspective to challenging business issues. Men and women see things differently. That real strength isn't possible when two men or two women face the same challenges.
- Household management and child care may be easier when working together in a home-based business.

Cons

- Living with someone in a marriage is strain enough. Are you sure you want to work with your spouse, too?
- If both husband and wife jump into the new venture, who brings home the bacon until the business builds? Financial demands and risks may be much greater when neither person has a steady income. And it's amazing how much one person can help, even after working forty hours in another job. Steady income is critical if capital is limited.

If You Do It, Here's How

As Bootstrap Entrepreneurs, if you do decide to start your business together, you must clearly define your roles. Analyze the strengths and weaknesses of each. Make a conscious decision about who will be responsible for which activity. Decide who will be responsible for advertising, sales, buying, bookkeeping, customer complaints, planning, and budgets. Obviously, the other person is always supportive and will pinch-hit if necessary. But consciously knowing who is responsible for what will add immensely to your opportunity for success.

Next, avoid controversial business discussion at home in the evening. Sure, you're always communicating. That's normal. But if you differ on any issue, look at each other, smile, and hold it over for tomorrow at the office. You will communicate better, you will make a better decision, and you will be kinder to your marriage. There are enough strains in marriage. Don't let business issues add to them.

Here's another constructive idea that took Valerie and I years to work out. Try having regular meetings together, weekly or monthly. Pretend you are staff employees with another organization. This way you have a definite time to deal with tough issues. Don't rely only on snatches of information you exchange in the car or over the dinner table. Set up formal meetings for formal discussions, and give the business the attention it deserves.

Chapter 16

When Is the Right Time to Start a New Business?

There is never a right time. There are always problems and barriers to stop you if you let them. Life blesses you with these challenges to see if you deserve the success you say you want. If you intend to be a Bootstrap Entrepreneur, take action now. That action does not mean you must give up your job and blindly launch a business on a wing and a prayer.

It does mean to begin immediately on your business start-up plan. Investigate competition. Decide on the product or service you will offer. Learn what your customers want. Build up your savings. And most of all, set a deadline for when you will make your first sale.

Today, right here, right now, at this very instant, is your personal moment of truth. Will you become a Bootstrap Entrepreneur: yes or no? Your decision is the most crucial step you will take in your entire entrepreneurial career. You may accept the challenge or reject it.

But do it now! There will never be a better time.

If You Say Yes

If you accept this challenge today, this is a red-letter day in your life! Record it in your notebook. Write it in the margin of this book. Keep it with you always—the exact day, hour, and minute. Why? Because the instant you write down your firm decision—and put a deadline on it—your new future begins.

If You Say No

However, if you reject this opportunity, be assured that you are doing the right thing. At this point in time, you are not prepared to accept the challenge of independence. Whatever fear is holding you back, it would sabotage your success were you to act. Think on it. Identify it. Give a name to the impenetrable barrier that stops you. Whatever it is, you must first master that barrier before you can master yourself and your success in business.

Begin today to attract the forces you need so you do not live in fear forever. Failure is not so bad. Many who tried did not succeed the first time. But not to try is to forever wonder what might have been.

This is an action book for the Bootstrap Entrepreneur. At this moment, decisive action is required. If you have taken the action required, continue. If not, close this book now. Save it for another time when you are ready to make important decisions about your life and your future.

Part 4

Choosing Your Business

Chapter 17

The Right One for You

Choosing the business that's right for you is the most important business decision you will make. The issue isn't simply about money, although many think it is. Getting caught up in money issues—how much money does it take, how much money will it make—is easy. But the bigger issue is *you!*

Every person is different by nature and by nurture. For some, risk is fearful; for others, it's fun. For some, creativity is easy; for others, it's a struggle. For some, counting inventory and keeping records are satisfying, pleasurable tasks; for others, they are impossible chores they don't like and won't do.

Yes, money is important. The economics of return on investment and reward for your effort are essential, but money is the second issue. You—your likes, your dislikes, your temperament, and your talent—are far more important in choosing the right business for you.

In this part, I'll guide you to narrow your choices but pay particular attention to 23, "Be Passionate"; 24, "What Do You

Enjoy?"; and 25, "What Do You Do Well?" When you go with the natural flow of your feelings and not just the logic of economics, your potential for success is heightened all the more.

Chapter 18

Money vs. Time

There are two scarce resources when it comes to life and to business: money and time. When it comes to a new business, money is usually more scarce. Later, as the business succeeds, time becomes more scarce.

Your resources of money and time may determine the type of business you enter. Your money resource is governed by savings plus your ability to borrow plus supplier credit. Your time resource depends on your job, your family situation, and your experience in maximizing the effectiveness of each hour you invest. Your ability to borrow is based on your reputation, integrity, and talent to convince people you can do what you say you will do. And a little collateral helps.

As you read, consider your options. Constantly think about your resources of money and time and how you balance them to your best benefit.

. . . .

*"Practically all great fortunes
began in the form of compensation
for personal services, or from the
sale of ideas. What else, except
ideas and personal services, would
one not possessed of property have
to give in return for riches?"*
—*Napoleon Hill*

. . . .

Chapter 19

Knowledge vs. Inventory

Inventory is expensive!

It ties up capital. It becomes obsolete. It gets stolen. It goes stale. It rots when the refrigerator breaks. It gets wet when floods come or pipes break. It gets smoky and burns in a fire. Do all you can to avoid inventory—and the rent to store it and the money to insure it.

While almost every business needs equipment or tools to do business—a truck, shelving, file cabinets, a fax machine, and often much more—not every business needs inventory. Professionals—architects, lawyers, and dentists—don't. Sales reps—brokers and insurance agents—don't. Most services—secretaries and carpet cleaners—don't.

Note the common denominator of those that don't require inventory: knowledge! The idea goes further. Even if inventory is needed, knowledge can keep it to a minimum. Knowledge can come from your skill, experience, and resourcefulness. It can come from your computer.

It can come from reading this page and your decision to do everything you can to keep inventory to a minimum.

. . . .

*Substitute Knowledge
for Inventory.*

. . . .

Chapter 20

The Trend Is Your Friend

When you start a new business, try to be in the early stages of a long-term growing trend but not necessarily the very first ones. Wait. There's time to be sure it's not a fad, even if the salesperson tells you there isn't. Consider the big picture—the economy and society at large. Some business products are classic and with us always, but others are affected by changes in technology, ecology, and sociology.

For example, clothing will be with us always. And perhaps cigarette smoking. However, the 1990s may not be a good time to enter the fur business or the cigarette vending machine business. On the other hand, it might be a very good time to start a business related to the environment or computer technology.

Also, don't make a negative decision based on a negative short-term trend, such as a dip in the economy. That will change in a year or two. Instead, be aware of trends for the next ten or twenty years. That's easy to say, not easy to do. Here are some ideas.

Peter Drucker, a famous management consultant, tells us

in his book *Managing for Results,* "The deliberate commit-ment of present resources to an unknown and unknowable future is the specific function of the entrepreneur in the term's original meaning." And if we are alert, we can often sense a "future that has already happened."

What does that mean, a "future that has already hap-pened"? It means that an educator who was aware that more than 75 million babies were born in the twenty years follow-ing World War II did not have to be a genius to figure out what was coming. As the first wave of baby boomers entered kindergarten, the educator could predict with certainty the number who would later enter high school and college. It was a future that had already happened.

That future is still happening today. Baby boomers are maturing. The break point for an important human "pas-sage," as Gail Sheehy calls it, is age forty. The first baby boomer turned forty in 1986—only a few years ago. They will continue to turn forty until the year 2004 and will con-tinue growing older for another forty years after that. An executive friend made this astounding observation: "Baby boomers are the first generation in the history of the world that have more parents than children."

What does this fact tell the thoughtful Bootstrap Entre-preneur? Well, any business having to do with needs of mid-dle-aged and older people is likely to have a huge market in the future. In the 1970s, baby boomers were snapping up transistor radios and Levi's jeans faster than stores could stock them. Now, in the early 1990s, baby boomers are start-ing to settle down. They have gone through the phase of designer names on their shirts and shoes and purses—the gaudy show-it-all, tell-it-all look.

The recession of the early 1990s brought a sea change in spending habits. It's pretty safe to say boomers are making a long-term shift in attitudes to treasure more permanent, higher value, and less-showy products.

How could that affect which business a Bootstrap Entre-preneur commits the future to? Think about it. What will boomers care about in the future? They will care about their health, their appearance, and their comfort inside the home. They already care about quality and service. And for the next ten years, they will care about babies. There is now an echo baby boom demographers didn't expect. It will be a significant business opportunity for years to come.

For example, health and fitness will be an explosive market as baby boomers begin turning fifty in 1996. Already health clubs and health food stores and restaurants are booming. There is even a to-your-door mobile fitness business in southern California that brings a gymnasium to your home along with a personal trainer. The trainer helps affluent aging boomers build strength, improve appearance, and prolong life. Business that caters to the over fifty market will have twenty-five to fifty years of strong growth to come.

If you, a Bootstrap Entrepreneur, can hitch a wagon to a favorable trend, you will surely increase your odds of success. To learn more about trends in the nineties and beyond, try these excellent books, *Megatrends 2000* and *The Popcorn Report* (details in the Bibliography).

Chapter 21

Businesses to Avoid

Avoid the pitfalls of a glamour business—you know, ones that look like a lot of fun but don't make much money. Things like independent travel agent, music teacher, and almost any artistic endeavor would fall into this category. Why? Because the musician and the artist concentrate on the pleasure and excellence of their crafts instead of marketing to build a business. Sure, there are exceptions but beware.

Other examples of the glamour syndrome include cute little gift shops, fancy stationery stores, charming dress and accessory shops, and other businesses that retail beautiful and interesting things. You just knew it would be so-o-o much fun to be around such pretty things. And you could go on buying trips. And talk to wonderful customers with exquisite taste. Wouldn't that be fun! Of course, it would be fun. But it wouldn't make money.

Gun shops, auto customizing, and boating-related shops also fall in this category. These businesses serve inner urges of the owners for pleasurable activity rather than careful thought in business planning.

The business motive is not profit. Merchandising, promotion, and finding customers are often the last things these owners think about. Yes, it's fun to own a glamour business or a beautiful boutique until the rent is due and the bills pour in. Then it's not fun anymore.

I wish I could tell you how many gift shops, card shops, design studios, yarn stores, boutiques, and other fun and pretty businesses I've seen start up one year and screech to a halt the next.

How do you spot a profitless glamour business? One of the best ways is to ask yourself where the focus is—on buying or on selling, on doing operations work or on finding customers. Everyone wants to be a buyer. Hardly anyone wants to sell. But when you have your own business, the money, dear Bootstrap Entrepreneur, is made from selling, not from buying.

Chapter 22

Types
of Business

As you consider different businesses, you should know that only two types attract two-thirds of Bootstrap Entrepreneurs (The other one-third of business start-ups are in mail order, manufacturing, wholesaling, and other fields.):

1. Service businesses, either home based or location based
2. Retail stores/restaurants, generally location based

So, let's look more at service and retail/restaurant needs that represent about 2 million new start-ups per year.

Service Business

In a service business, you may be able to start from your home or in a low-cost location. Also, a service business should require little or no inventory. That will cut your initial investment substantially. In fact, a service business may require as little as $1,000 to $2,000 and generally no more than $30,000 to get started. You may not even need employees if you start the business yourself.

Surprisingly, a service business started with low investment may be just as profitable as others requiring $50,000, $100,000, or even more to begin. That sounds terrific. So why doesn't everybody do it? The downside to a service business is this: you must go out and find your customers. You can't expect them to come to you. For example, if you start a retail store in a shopping center, customers are all around. Some may walk in and buy from you. Your major marketing cost is the high rent you pay. On the other hand, to succeed in a service business, you should be a pleasant, smiling person with a positive attitude. You should have the personal drive to get out and meet people. You should enjoy serving others. If this sounds like your personality (or you are willing to develop it), seriously consider a service business.

Retail Store/Restaurant

The main feature of a retail or restaurant business is that it has a physical location. If the products and location are right, the customers will flock in. Then it becomes your job to see they are served promptly and pleasantly.

While it will require a higher investment than a service business, a retail business is tangible. That is, you can see the sign outside, you can walk into the inviting surroundings, and you can touch and feel the merchandise. For these reasons a successful retail business may command a premium when you want to sell it later on. Because they demand inventory, store fixtures, and remodeling, expect retail/restaurant businesses to require from $50,000 to $250,000 to start (and more).

The traps and pitfalls of a retail business are legion. It is easy to pick the wrong location or the wrong products, or to select a space that is too big or too small. The revenue potential in a retail business is unknown, but the costs are certain.

Another disadvantage is the long hours of being open evenings and weekends.

Still, retail may be an appropriate answer for you. Minimize your risk of loss by following carefully the ideas you find later in part 5. Also, seek good advice if a retail store or restaurant is your business dream.

Chapter 23

Be Passionate

You may already have a good idea for a business you would like. About four out of five people who go into a new business already have experience with the type of product or service they're going to market. Or they're at least familiar with it from a hobby or pastime. Others get their ideas from a family business or friends or relatives. Only about one out of ten chances into something unexpected.

My wife, Valerie, has some sound advice on the business you choose: be passionate! Choose a business you believe in, one where you can express your personal values, one where you can contribute to others so you feel good inside. The best business is one you enjoy and customers enjoy. When you combine your passion for your business with your passion to make it succeed, you're guaranteed to win. No one can coach you to have passion. But if you have it, you can be coached to success.

. . . .

*Demand the best from yourself and
for your customers.*

. . . .

Chapter 24

What Do You Enjoy?

Consider a hobby or pastime you enjoy as an option for a business. What do you like to do? Read? Consider a bookstore. Snow ski? Think about clothing, equipment, maybe transportation to the lift. Are you a fastidious home cleaner? Consider it for others. Do you enjoy children? A child-care service, toddler clothing store, car pool for money. Are you fascinated by automobiles? Auto parts, repair, customizing, restoring.

Make a list of all the things you enjoy doing. Then start with the top two. Brainstorm with a friend about all the possibilities. Look in the yellow pages for listings of businesses related to your interest. (If your city is less than 1 million population, order a phone book from a larger city in your region. Cost is nominal.)

Let ideas roll around your mind for a few weeks. Bounce them off people you know who are positive and supportive. Avoid naysayers. There's plenty of time for that later. In the gestation stage, make no judgments about what won't work; look only for reasons why it might work. In part 5, you'll study how to check out your ideas to see if they're viable.

Chapter 25

What Do You Do Well?

You probably have a job now. Maybe a career you studied for and are experienced in. The first question to ask yourself is, Do I want to change my career or to find a way to use my career skills in my own business? Sometimes we get soured by a work environment or day-to-day activities we don't like. But how would you feel if you just got rid of the parts you don't like and could find a way to do more of what you do like? Would you still want to change careers?

However, if what you're doing now is not an answer for your future—even with adjustments—let's take a different tack. Start by writing your résumé. Go all the way back. List everything you've done for money. When you finish, you may be surprised at all you've done. You probably have more skills and experience than you would give yourself credit for without thinking it through.

Now look over all the things you've done. Which ones did you enjoy? Did you know a coworker in a different job who was doing something you found interesting and you know you could do it, too, with a little training or experi-

ence? Use your résumé and your knowledge about other related jobs to make a list of things you know you could do for
money, even if you were working for someone else.

Then expand your ideas to jobs you've observed or heard
about, jobs you think you might like to do. Think of it this
way. If a business will pay money for these jobs, chances are,
an independent business can be designed to make money for
a creative entrepreneur.

In a nutshell, consider the job skills you have or those
you want to learn. Even though you may not want to use
these skills working for someone else, perhaps there's a nug-
get of an idea to consider if you were working for yourself.
Think about the possibilities a few days. See what comes to
mind.

Chapter 26

Do What Big Business Can't

Big business does some things better than small business —raise and use large amounts of capital; buy, warehouse, and distribute large inventories of products; and achieve mass market awareness with millions of consumers.

Small business does some things better than big business —adapt to local market conditions; give extra care, dedication, and commitment to customers; make immediate decisions to assure satisfaction; use superior skill and experience to solve problems; and add a personal touch no big business can equal.

As you consider things you like to do and job skills you do well, think how you can beat big business at things it can't do. Usually, your edge will be in one of these areas:

1. Unique, custom, or nonstandard products and services. Big business wants things uniform. It hates the unusual that doesn't fit the system. Getting an okay on a small variation may have to go through six layers of management.
2. Knowledge, skill, and experience. Big business is al-

ways short of skilled talent. The best are promoted quickly. Then customers no longer get the benefit of their skill. Instead, they get a junior replacement you can run circles around.

3. Fast delivery. Big business consolidates inventory in regional shipping points that may be several days by truck from your customers. Even worse, the order system is a nightmare—salesperson to order desk to credit approval to warehouse to trucking company. And if somebody goes on vacation, the order will probably sit in a stack for a week. You can easily beat that.

4. On-the-spot eyeball analysis. You can go out to the project, identify a problem by using your superior experience, and make an immediate decision because you own the business. Big business's response is laughable. I don't have to tell you that.

5. Flexibility. Big business requires everyone to follow a foot-thick policy manual. An entrepreneur makes policy on the spot. Look for customers who need exceptions as a normal course of business and you'll eat big business for lunch.

Where can small business shine and outmaneuver big business? I've listed some examples. I'm sure you can add more.

Things related to home . . .

- Remodeling
- Lawn care
- Pool service
- Upholstery
- Landscaping
- Handyman service
- Housecleaning
- House-sitting
- Window treatments
- Floor covering, sales and installation
- Kitchen remodeling
- Custom stereo products and installation
- Plumbing

- Electrical services
- Window washing
- Pet care
- Interior design

Things related to apparel . . .

- Dry cleaning shop
- Unique dress store
- Specialized accessories
- Sewing, tailoring, alterations
- Wardrobe advice

Things related to business . . .

- Typing, secretarial service
- Packing, shipping, receiving service
- Office machine repair
- Janitorial service
- Personnel agency
- Accounting
- Consulting

Again, look at the index in a yellow pages directory. You'll find dozens of businesses where the independent entrepreneur has a big edge over big business.

Don't let big business intimidate you. Gobble it up.

Chapter 27

Watch
the News

Every day a new business is profiled in the news. A new business that works—that is, one that's been around at least a year—may be novel and needed in your area. Watch the business and financial segments on local and network TV shows and CNN.

Read the business section in a major daily. The *Wall Street Journal* runs the feature "Enterprise" every day on the first or second page of the second section. If you don't want to pay $140 a year for a subscription, stop by your library once a week.

Watch for a new idea that rings a bell with you. Then check it out and get more information. Call the public information office if you learn about it from radio or TV. Try the reporter direct if it's in the newspaper. It may be better to wait a week or two if the feature was national. The business may be flooded with inquiries. Oftentimes a featured business will be a franchise because it seeks media attention to expand the system. Don't get hung up if you get no response immediately. Keep bugging the person until you find out

what you want to know. Some franchisors are good operators but poor franchise salespeople, especially if they are
new. Give 'em a break—and yourself, too.

Of course, franchise or otherwise, your checkout procedure will be the same as for any business you consider (we'll
cover that in the next part).

Chapter 28

The Best
Idea of All

Find a business you like that's twenty, two hundred, or two thousand miles away, one where somebody else has done all the pioneering (a pioneer is someone with arrows in his back).

It's much better to be the first in your area with a new business than to be the first to pioneer a new business. You always want to learn from the person who made all the start-up mistakes the first year or two. So, how to go about it?

1. Keep your eyes open when you travel. Watch for the unusual and appealing. Most of all, see whether customers are coming in and whether they are buying.

2. Subscribe to one or two out-of-town daily papers. We've already talked about checking news and feature stories in the business sections. But go beyond that. Check the ads. Thumb through the display ads and the classifieds, especially in the "Services Directory," which most papers have today.

Also watch for "advertorials." These are paid advertisements that look like editorial feature stories. New small businesses tend to use these ads because they have a story to tell. Their concept may be hard to get across in a promotional discount ad.

3. Once again, thumb through the yellow pages. They cost so little ($5 to $15 each), you can order a half dozen books for a small investment. The good news is that you can use out-of-town directories to get ideas about which business to go into and also to check out the one you think you like. (More on this approach later.)

In summary, the best idea of all is to find a business you can enjoy that has proven itself somewhere else first, one that allows you to use your skills. Then be a hero in your area as you introduce it.

Part 5

Checking Out the Business You Like

Chapter 29

Importance of Checking It Out

As a Bootstrap Entrepreneur, you now have an idea about the business you want. You also have some idea about the products you want to offer. Once these ideas take shape, you must dig deeper.

After all, why would anyone consider investing thousands of dollars and many years into a new business before checking into it carefully? I don't know the answer, but I've seen it happen a hundred times. Don't let it happen to you as a responsible Bootstrap Entrepreneur. Instead, let's take a look at an orderly process to check out the type of business you want.

Chapter 30

Visit
Local
Businesses

Your first step is to visit other businesses in your area that offer similar products or services. If you're thinking about a card and gift shop, visit the card and gift shops in your area. Visit the greeting card departments in department stores, in grocery and drug stores, and in any other location you can find. Take notice of what you see.

At each location, calculate the rough square footage. Estimate the number of cards in a typical rack. Then count the racks. You will get an idea about how many cards are in inventory. Then estimate the average retail price of most of the cards, say $1.00 to $1.50. Now you can make a quick estimate of the retail value of the inventory you see, and you can do some figuring about inventory investment.

Of course, inventory at cost will be much less than inventory at retail. For any type of specialty shop, assume the wholesale cost is about half of retail. For large retail stores that sell at discount, cost may be only 33 to 40 percent less than retail. Once you have an estimate, write it down. Compare it to other stores you visit. Get a feel for the difference in inventory and investment between big and small stores.

Check Out Suppliers

Now look around the store for more things. Who are the suppliers? Most manufacturers have names on their products. Write their names in your handy notebook (you always have a notebook). Oftentimes these manufacturers will be represented by distributors whose names are not available. That doesn't matter now. You can find that out later.

Look around at the lighting, the displays, and the fixtures. Evaluate the signs. Note good ideas you see—and bad ones, too. Remember, the way something strikes you is pretty much how it will strike customers who come in the store. Also keep a section of your notebook for great ideas. As you become a more sensitive observer, you will want to list all the interesting things you see. Even more important, you will come up with your own inspired ideas. Yours are valuable. They will set your business apart from the competition.

Continue to check things out. As Yogi Berra said, "You can observe a lot just by watching." Watch how the clerks behave. Which are employees? Which is the manager or owner? Buy something for a couple of dollars. While the person is ringing it up at the cash register, engage in casual conversation. You want to ask questions and do some detective work.

Be Pleasant and Listen

Start off by saying, "This is a nice store. How long have you been here in business?" If the cashier is the owner, ask how the person got the idea to start such a beautiful business. If the clerk is an employee, ask who the owner is. Also ask how long the employee has worked there. Let whomever you're talking to know how impressed you are with the store. People will tell you lots of things you want to know when you're nice to them.

After thoroughly checking out several stores in your city,

you will probably form some ideas about how things work in this business. Things like how much floor space and how much back room space you'll need. What kind of location seems the best and what stores appear busiest. And why.

Chapter 31

Check Out Nonstore Businesses

It's easy to see how to check out a retail store, but how do you check out a business that doesn't have a store? It's not so difficult. The Bootstrap Entrepreneur will find there are two types of service businesses. One type charges for a consultation, such as a lawyer, a doctor, and sometimes an accountant or other professional.

The other type will provide an initial visit and an estimate without charge. Whatever service you are interested in —auto detailing, carpet cleaning, lawn and garden maintenance, tax service, or anything else—take a tip from leading businesses that hire professional shoppers to learn about competition. You can be your own competitive shopper. Simply present yourself as a customer and get estimates from several businesses. Naturally, you're going to be extra pleasant and ask plenty of questions.

How to Size Up Service Businesses

Start with the yellow pages. Keep your notebook handy. The first thing to notice is which businesses have the larger ads and which have the smaller ones. If you can, find last year's telephone book and, even better, the year before that. Chances are, the business with the largest ad one or two years ago is no longer a going concern. (It went broke spending too much money on advertising.) But verify whether that happened. Make a careful study of who is still around and who isn't. Talking to successful survivors will be enlightening. Talking to owners of businesses that folded may be even more so.

As you call each business, be aware of employees' telephone etiquette. Make notes of what you like and what you don't like. When the representative arrives to give you an estimate, mentally answer these questions: Did he show up on time? How is she dressed? How neat are the grooming and appearance? And most of all, how friendly is the attitude?

Watch how each representative gives the sales presentation. Yes, theoretically, it is just an estimate. But if the estimator is worth his salt, he will try to sell you on the idea of using the service. Jot information in your notebook about details of the estimate and also about ideas on the sales presentation.

What does she say? What things do you like and don't like? Especially notice whether the representative asks you questions and considers your ideas. Or instead does she just plunge headlong into telling you how great the company is?

After you review a half dozen representatives in the type of business you are contemplating, you will know who your strongest competitors are. You will have a basic idea about their pricing policies and the quality of their service. And you will know the competitive features of each business you may go up against later.

How do you know when enough is enough? When you

no longer hear anything new. Generally, after six to ten interviews, when two or three representatives in a row tell you the same things you've already heard, your investigation is finished.

It's time to go to the next step.

Chapter 32

Visit
Out-of-Town
Businesses

Select the largest city within a two- or three-hour drive from where you live. You are going out of town to visit more businesses similar to the one you plan to enter. Your card shop, for example. Why go to another city when you've just spent days visiting eight to ten different stores in your city?

Business owners away from your city will be more open in talking to you. You can discover inside details about how the industry works. You can learn who are the best suppliers. You can hear about excellent ideas that made a business successful.

If at all possible, get a yellow pages directory and a map for the city you're going to visit. Locate as many retailers as you possibly can on the map the night before you leave, up to a total of twenty. Twenty is the magic number you can visit in one day. Chances are, you'll find only four or five where the owner is in and will be able to take the time to talk to you.

Okay, let's stop a minute and talk about this adventure. Does it seem like a strange idea? Maybe something that is hard for you to do? Yes, I grant you, it is different. But that's what being a Bootstrap Entrepreneur is all about—doing things differently to save money and make profits faster. You will be amazed at what you uncover in just one or two days of diligent detective work. It may save you thousands of dollars in dead-end mistakes. It may show you ways to make thousands of dollars in added profit in a short time. Yes, this is a different approach, but you will find it most worthwhile.

You probably feel you are unfairly intruding on another business owner's time. Not at all. Entrepreneurs are pleased to talk about themselves. They want to tell you all their ideas —the ones that worked and the ones that didn't. If you are likable and pleasant, they will want to help you. They will take you under their wings and wish you well in your new venture. They will admire your gumption. They will respect you for the way you're checking out the business before you leap. If they are not pleasant and helpful, they are not leaders. You can rely on that based on my personal experience with over ten thousand prospecting interviewers.

Do It in One Day

If you have your map all laid out and leave your city by 6:00 or 7:00 A.M., you should be able to visit all twenty retailers and be back by sometime after dinner. Be sure to take your notebook and even a small tape recorder. Of course, you never make recordings without asking permission first. But you will be surprised after you have built up rapport, how many owners will not object if you want to record some of their most important comments.

When you have finished asking all your questions or as many as seem appropriate and comfortable, be sure to let the owners know how much you appreciate their time and their help. Tell them you'll be sure and write about whether you actually go into this business and how it works out.

Why not have a few gifts in your car? (Be creative. They need not be extravagant.) After an especially helpful interview, give the business owner a gift on the spot. Show your appreciation for the time spent with you. I guarantee the person will remember you forever, wish you luck, and offer assistance whenever you need it.

Your final question as you depart will be, "Would it be all right if I call you sometime in the future when I have a special question?" The answer will always be yes. Now the door is open for you to follow up with any points that come up later. No one will object to hearing from you once a month over the next two or three months. Because of your thank-you gift and your attitude, business owners will want to see you do well.

If you have a grand opening, be sure to invite them. Naturally, you will send a thank-you card and a follow-up letter about your progress and how much they contributed to your success.

Remember, as you're asking business owners questions, you will ask about suppliers, employees, and operation of the business itself. That's natural. But the really important question is, Where do the customers come from? The Bootstrap Entrepreneur knows the real business of business is not doing the business but finding business. Don't shortchange this vital topic.

Chapter 33

Questions
to Ask
Business Owners

To get your own ideas started, read through these suggested questions to ask business owners you interview. Feel free to add to this list.

For Local Business Owners

- How long have you been in business?
- Do you enjoy it?
- What do you like the best about the business?
- What are your hours?

For Out-of-Town Business Owners

- How did you happen to get into this business?
- Did it work out the way you expected?
- Would you do it again?
- What would you do differently if you had to do it all over again?
- What two ideas have been the best ones to help you get new customers?

- What do customers most like about your business?
- What are your *best* customers like? What income range, type of home, or other factors make them different from the others?
- If I were to open a store in another city, should it be larger or smaller?
- Would you recommend about the same type of merchandise?
- About how much should I spend on advertising?
- What would you estimate my total expenses should be each month?
- About how much would I have to sell each month to break even before taking a salary? (Note: Read 45, "Financial Planning," and use the Financial Planning Work Sheet on page 185.)
- Not including my living expense, about how much working capital would I need for the first three months? (Note: This is a loaded question. Do not expect an accurate answer. Most independent business owners have not made a careful analysis and will shoot from the hip.)
- What should I expect my sales to be at the end of the first three months? How about at the end of the first year and the second year?
- About how many customers each day will I need to make the level of sales I need?
- Are there any products you carry now that I won't need for the first year or so?
- Is there anything you don't carry that I should consider in the first year?
- What suppliers do you think I should try to work with? What is the name of the salesperson who covers this area? Do you have the person's telephone number?
- Are there any trade associations for this industry? What are the names? Phone? Do they have regional or national meetings? Where? (See 34, "Trade Associations, Shows, and Events.")

Chapter 34

Trade Associations, Shows, and Events

One of the first steps in checking out a business you like is contacting trade associations concerned with the products or services. Trade associations are extremely valuable. They publish monthly magazines with advertising by important suppliers. The magazines will feature profiles of successful independent business owners. You can learn much from what is reported in these magazines. Ask for back issues to give you a great source of fast information. Don't accept all you read as gospel, but it is added input for your mental computer.

Trade associations may also have research departments. Request all you can about the industry, retailers, and standard operating ratios for advertising, inventory, and profitability. A good association will have studies about average sales, number of employees, sales per square foot, profitability of typical businesses, and often a listing of leading retailers throughout the nation. What a wonderful source of information for a new Bootstrap Entrepreneur considering a similar business! Phone these owners wherever they are. Most will be flattered to answer your specific questions.

Trade associations may organize annual or semiannual conventions and events. There may be training conferences, workshops, and supplier exhibitions. They are wonderful opportunities to learn about the industry even before you make the final commitment to enter a new venture.

Chapter 35

How to Get in a Trade Show

So, how do you get into a trade show since it is for the trade? It's really simple. Pick a business name. Base it on your own name for a start. Have a small quantity of business cards printed at low cost (only about $10 or $15). Use your home telephone number and address. An added touch would be to get a sales tax number, which costs nothing in most states.

Armed with your business card and sales tax number, you will likely gain entrance to most any trade show relevant to your business. Always tell people the truth. You are starting a new business and do not have it fully organized. If you talk to a supplier about setting up an account, insist on being COD. That way, you avoid having your account turned down because of a credit investigation. It is also good business sense for the new Bootstrap Entrepreneur.

Be open with sales representatives and suppliers. Some will welcome your inquiry. They may encourage you to go into business and want to sell to you. Others may discourage you and be uninterested in your business. Don't worry about that now. The point of meeting suppliers at trade shows is to gain information about the business you're going into. Don't worry at this point about how to obtain merchandise.

To get the names of trade associations for the business you want, ask other retailers. Also ask the research desk at the public library. Reference books are available for this purpose. Check out the associations. Call each one. You'll be glad you did.

Chapter 36

Decision Time

Once you have interviewed owners of similar businesses, both in your city and in a distant city, contacted relevant trade associations, read back issues of trade magazines, attended a trade show or event and, of course, kept a voluminous record of ideas in your trusty notebook, you should be ready to make a decision.

You should have an excellent grasp of the business by now. You should have discovered some sobering ideas along with some exciting ones.

Possibly, you're more frightened than you thought you might be, or possibly, you're more excited. Whichever extreme you feel, try to balance it. Remember, reality is somewhere in between. Also remember, if you're getting cold feet, no one said it would be easy to be a Bootstrap Entrepreneur.

Hundreds, thousands, yes, even millions of other entrepreneurs were once just as frightened as you are now. They have paved the way to make your job easier. They have survived and prospered. Reassure yourself you're going about things in the right way. Believe in yourself. You can surely do as well, or better, than many others who have gone before you.

Chapter 37

If You Still Have Doubts

At this point there are not many more ways to check out a business, but here are two ideas. One is to try before you buy. If you are still uncertain, go to work for someone who has a business like the one you want. Get a leave of absence for three months. Take a cut in pay. Even work for free if you must.

If there is any doubt in your mind about the way the business should work, or whether you will prosper at it, simply go to work for someone else in the same field. You will learn an immense amount. Within thirty to sixty days, you will have a good grasp about whether the business is right for you. Remember, this idea is not for every Bootstrap Entrepreneur, only for those with tremendous uncertainty about whether they can make the business succeed.

The second idea to consider is whether you might be better off in network marketing or a franchise instead of going it alone. Let's explore these possibilities in the next two chapters.

Chapter 38

Network Marketing— Yes or No?

Network marketing is a contemporary term for multilevel management organizations (often referred to as MLM). Some people think these are pyramid sales organizations. That is not true for the reputable ones. A pyramid sales scheme is one where the new representative pays a fee for the right to represent the company rather than pays for the products themselves.

Of course, the most well-known success story is the Amway Corporation. Many others, such as Herbalife, Nuskin, and some lesser known companies, have borrowed pages from Amway's book.

The essentials for success in such an organization are that the representative has three functions: (1) to be a user of the products, (2) to sell products retail to friends and others, and (3) to recruit more representatives.

Through overrides and bonuses, individuals who can recruit and motivate a sales team can make a substantial income. The upper 1 percent may exceed $100,000 a year in profits. Many individuals lured by low up-front investment and high income potential enter the field of network marketing. Some succeed. Many do not.

Is network marketing a valid option for the Bootstrap Entrepreneur? The answer is yes for two reasons. First, you may be one of the exceptional persons who build a profitable business. Second, and more likely, you will find the experience an excellent training ground.

Expect to learn positive business attitudes, sound sales techniques, methods to deal with rejection, skills in recruiting, and ways to motivate others. These and other ideas will be helpful to you in the years to come, regardless of the business you eventually find as a life career.

The same can be said for most direct sales organizations. The Bootstrap Entrepreneur will benefit from sales experience with cookware, encyclopedias, insurance, cosmetics, and other products.

Is direct sales experience a requirement for success? No, but it will add to your skills in building a new business and leading employees. If you join such an organization, follow everything you're told, even if it's not your normal self. You may benefit immensely for years to come in ways you would never predict.

Chapter 39

Franchise— Yes or No?

Having been a franchisor and member of the International Franchise Association for almost twenty years, I believe in franchising. At the same time, I know it is not right for everyone.

What is a franchise? Lots of books will give you a detailed definition. But the basic idea is simply this: a *franchisor* owns a trademark that may be well known to the public. Rights to use the trademark are sold for a franchise fee and ongoing royalties. In addition to granting rights to use the trademark, most franchisors have a business format to follow. This format, or system, can increase the likelihood of success by the *franchisee*. You can find many books about franchising and its technical, legal basis at your library.

But what you may not find in library books is the reality of what you get for your money. It really boils down to this: you are buying *time*. With a proven system, you should achieve a higher level of sales and profits more quickly than you would likely achieve on your own. In other words, without a franchise, you might eventually, over a period of years, learn almost everything a franchisor would show you.

Value of Being Independent

More freedom and control

- Don't have to conform to policies or managers
- Stand entirely on your own decisions

Lower up-front investment

- Pay no franchise fee
- Start smaller as an option

No royalty on sales

- Have potentially lower expense

Instead, by paying a franchise fee generally from $2,000 to $20,000, you should expect to learn the business much faster. Within one year, you may learn things that would take you three or more years to learn on your own. The franchise fee may or may not include equipment, supplies, promotional materials, and other items you need for your start-up. But generally, you would need all these things whether you buy a franchise or do it on your own.

The real questions to consider when it comes to the initial franchise fee are these: Can you avoid enough costly mistakes, and can you start your business faster, to justify the initial fee? The next question deals with ongoing royalties. Royalties and advertising fees may run from as little as 4 or 5 percent to as much as 20 or 30 percent in some service businesses. Assume a fairly typical fee base of about 10 percent. Now you have a different question to ponder: How much in *extra* sales and in *extra* gross profit can you achieve because you are a member of a franchise, as compared to doing it yourself?

The idea of getting extra sales is probably easy to understand. That is, through the franchisor's system and name reputation, will you sell a few more customers each month than you would likely get on your own? If you can get more sales, that in itself may pay the cost of royalties.

The next point to compare is gross profit. The idea of gross profit may be new to you. Gross profit is the amount of leftover money you keep *after* paying wholesale cost for products you sell (or direct labor cost in a service business). A franchisor should help you increase your gross profit in two different ways. First of all, the franchisor should help you buy your products for less than you would pay on your own. The savings may seem small, possibly only 5 to 10 percent, but by the end of the year, small savings add up to a lot.

The second point, which is often overlooked, is that the franchised business may command a premium in pricing compared to independent businesses because customers like to do business with a national name. They appreciate the added security. And oftentimes there are guarantees or other assurances of quality and satisfaction. The result is, customers will pay a premium price for added security.

You must decide whether the franchise company you are looking at can truly help you achieve higher sales in a shorter period of time and higher gross profits on your sales. *It may not be able to do that.* You need to use your judgment on this point.

On the other hand, if the franchisor *can* help you increase retail sales and gross profit, the royalty fees it charges may be a good value. You may enjoy more net profit for yourself even after paying royalties. Remember, it's what you keep for yourself that counts—not what you pay out. Consider the added security of a proven system plus frequent meetings with other franchisees where you can exchange ideas, and you may conclude that investment in a franchise is worthwhile.

Finally, consider your temperament to work with others. Can you learn? Can you follow a system? And who will be

Value of Becoming a Franchisee

Time

- Grow faster with a proven system and marketing plan

Risk reduction

- Avoid losing money or making mistakes others made

Advertising

- Proven promotions
- Layouts, design, copy
- Budget guidelines

Support and guidance

- Franchisor's management
- Other franchisees

Group buying

- Initial equipment
- Supplies
- Products you sell

Name recognition

- Consumer credibility
- Potential awareness in your area

your mentor? If your direct supervisor is a good leader, skilled in bringing out the best in the team, you may find that is one of the most significant benefits of a franchise affiliation.

As a Bootstrap Entrepreneur, you want to enjoy fulfill-ment, satisfaction, and healthy operating profits. Explore and decide for yourself whether these are best achieved within a franchise organization or independently on your own.

Of course, if you seriously consider a franchise, go through the exact checkout procedure with the company's franchisees that you did with other similar businesses in your city and outside your city. Making telephone calls to franchisees is a beginning. But definitely see a handful of franchisees and ask them the same detailed questions you were provided earlier.

Part 6

Get Ready

Chapter 40

The Countdown Begins

As a Bootstrap Entrepreneur, you have now acted on the two most critical decisions in your business career:

1. You have made the *commitment* to definitely start your own business.
2. You have chosen the *direction* for the kind of business it will be.

I urge you to set a deadline now for when you will begin your business. It may be a month or a year but set the time now. The difference between a wish and a goal is a deadline. So, stop wishing and start acting!

By the way, if you are still working, don't quit. Hang on to your job and your income until the last possible moment. Even with a full-time job, you can complete the remaining parts of this book within thirty days. If you are not working now, you will need income soon. So, get with it! Begin your business as quickly as you can.

. . . .

*A Bootstrap Entrepreneur keeps the
money coming in.*

. . . .

Chapter 41

Your "Delicious Difference"

Once you decide the kind of business to own, figure out how you will set yourself apart from competitors. You must give your business a competitive edge! This "delicious difference" will be the foundation of your marketing plan and the basis for your competitive success.

Fortunately, the difference doesn't have to be great. The Bootstrap Entrepreneur understands the principle of the slight edge. It takes only a slight edge over competitors to make a big difference in results. Witness the Kentucky Derby where the first-place horse may win by a nose, yet first place takes tens of thousands of dollars more than second place. What a payoff for a small difference!

Next Memorial Day, observe the results of the Indianapolis 500 auto race. At the end of five hundred miles, one driver will take the checkered flag for first place. Generally, less than thirty seconds later the number two driver will cross the start-finish line. What is the difference in payoff these few seconds make after racing five hundred miles?

The 1992 Memorial Day race is a good example. After

some three hours of race time, Al Unser, Jr., took the black-and-white checkered flag less than one car length ahead of Scott Goodyear for a razor-thin edge of .0043 second. Unser's winnings were $1,244,184. Goodyear took less than half with $609,333. That made a difference of $634,851 for a difference in time of less than one-one hundredth of a second!

Yes, a slight edge can lead to a big payoff. What should your slight edge be? It may be price, although that is not recommended. It may be faster delivery. It may be better quality. It may be happier, more courteous, and caring employees. It may be quicker follow-up or a larger assortment or more convenience. Whatever your slight edge is, do it, promote it, and stick to it.

Someone once said,

> There are three fundamentals a small business can offer its customers:
> 1. Best price
> 2. Best quality
> 3. Best service
> Select any two!

You cannot be the best at everything. No business owner can offer the best of all three. But you might be best at two.

Let's look at some examples of what other businesses have done to add a slight edge to beat competition. In recent years Wal-Mart has become the number one retailer in the world, surpassing Sears and Kmart.

While Wal-Mart's entire corporate culture is a competitive edge, one of the most visible reminders is the Wal-Mart greeter. Each one smiles and says hello to every person who enters the store. The greeter hands the customer a market basket and offers to be of service. What a pleasing extra touch for a discount store.

Another wonderful example is Nordstrom. It is making retail history with friendly, attentive sales representatives. Each one will go the extra mile to serve you. Then add the ambiance of a tuxedo-clad pianist. Light classic and Broadway tunes reverberate through the store with a feeling of richness. The Nordstrom edge is the envy of every department store in America. Nordstrom doesn't claim the lowest prices in town. But it does provide a shopping experience second to none in retailing.

What about the grocery store where kids get free lollipops? Or the dentist who sends you a thank-you card after each visit? Or the Marriott Hotel concierge who gets you tickets to a Broadway show? Or the automobile dealer who calls you back to be sure your car was serviced properly? These are all examples of a slight edge that becomes a competitive edge to win customer loyalty.

Ask yourself what is missing in your industry. Think about all the stores you visited when you checked out your business. Was there anything missing as to price, quality, service, convenience, follow-up, guarantee, attention-getting displays, a pleasing environment? What can you do differently? What can you do better? What would your customers appreciate? Every time you visit a business—any business— ask yourself what things you like and what things you don't like. Chances are, you can learn something for your business almost everywhere you go.

Make your decision about the slight edge to give your business a "delicious difference." Then put it in writing. Put it on signs, brochures, and everything that tells customers about your business. Be sure your employees know what you stand for, and be sure they tell it to every customer and every person they meet. Then someday, the slight edge in your small business may lead you to become a big business. Wal-Mart and Nordstrom did it. Why can't you?

Chapter 42

Mission
and Purpose

What is the fundamental purpose of your business? In terms of benefits to the customer, what do you intend to do? How do you define your business? Your mission should be captured in a statement of purpose. To continue our card shop example, a mission statement might read like the one I've included here:

The Mission of ABC Card Shop
It is our intent to provide an outstanding selection of high-quality greeting cards and gift items for the discriminating customer. We will, at all times, maintain a comfortable, inviting environment for your shopping experience.

Our sales associates are committed to providing you pleasant, courteous, personal attention to every reasonable need and absolute satisfaction with every purchase. Please advise Mrs. Mary Kramer, the owner, if we ever fall short of this commitment to you.

Such a mission statement should be on framed parchment or a quality sign or brass plate. It should be visible in at least three locations throughout the store, including the cash register where people wait in line to be served.

How will displaying this statement benefit you? Most of all, it will help you crystallize in your mind the purpose of your business. Next, it will clearly communicate your purpose to employees, suppliers, contractors, and customers. It is one more way to stay focused on your purpose and to establish your leadership.

Chapter 43

Statement
of Values

Why does your small business need a statement of values? Every business is a personal extension of the founder's philosophy. Ask yourself,

- What do I stand for in my customer dealings?
- What do I believe in?
- What do I want people to know about my business?
- Am I committed to excellence in quality or excellence in price? (You probably cannot do both.)
- Am I committed to an exceptional product assortment—a broad choice for every customer?
- Will I treat each customer as an individual with extra attention?
- Will I strive for reliability in all I do? Will I deliver promptly on the day and hour scheduled?
- Will my employees be in uniform? Will they be non-smokers? Will they attend to details and clean up after giving service? Will they be smiling, courteous, and efficient?

- Will my staff and I be among the most expert and professional people in the field?
- Will I guarantee the satisfaction of every customer I serve?
- Will I go the extra mile in handling complaints and miscues of service, always giving the customer the benefit of the doubt?

What do you believe in? What will you stand for? Whatever it is, write it down and be sure your employees and your customers know your philosophy.

Does every independent business take this step? Absolutely not. That's one thing that will set you, a Bootstrap Entrepreneur, apart from the rest. It is not an easy exercise. Writing a statement of values takes commitment and professionalism. But it is vital.

Through your statement of values, you will tell customers, suppliers, employees, and all who come in contact with your business what you, as owner, stand for. And your standing will be a little taller in their eyes. It will give you charisma and magnetism. It will attract reliable people to follow your leadership and steady customers to stay with you a lifetime.

Four Ways to Increase Customers

Advertising

- Newspaper
- Yellow pages
- TV; radio
- Direct mail
- Fliers
- Other

Activities

- Phone calls
- Prospecting homes and businesses
- Seminars or events

Public relations

- Press releases
- Charity tie-ins
- Public speaking
- Newsletter

Follow up past customers
A BEST OPPORTUNITY

- Thank-you notes
- Appreciation Day
- Personal phone calls and visits

Chapter 44

Marketing Plan

It is time to address the most important of all elements in your business: how you will find customers.

The Bootstrap Entrepreneur knows that marketing is the number one challenge to be mastered. When you sell enough customers at the right price, success is virtually assured. Hundreds of books have been written on marketing and sales. In no way can we cover these subjects in a few paragraphs. However, we will identify the most critical points to consider and where you can learn more.

Your first marketing objective is to create awareness. Potential customers should know the name of your store, they should know the products and services you sell, and they should consider you when they need a product you offer.

When you have a retail store, the location itself is one way to achieve awareness. Be sure your signage is strong, attractive, and absolutely clear about what products you sell. In addition to your store location (or if you do not have a retail store), there are only three known ways to create awareness for a new business:

1. Advertising
2. Personal efforts
3. Publicity

One of the best sources on how to accomplish them affordably is the book *Guerilla Marketing Attack* by Jay Conrad Levinson. As a manager, you need to begin your marketing plan by figuring out your advertising budget. Decide immediately how much you will spend on advertising. A guideline for many businesses is to budget 10 to 15 percent of your first-year sales goal. Then reevaluate at six months and twelve months. For example, budget about $800 to $1,200 per month to sell $100,000 your first year. Next, determine what personal efforts you will make and what you will do to get publicity. Get these ideas crystal clear in your mind.

Then, think of the results you will expect—that is, the number of customers you will sell in your first three months in business. Make guesses, even if you don't know what to expect. At the end of ninety days, you can evaluate your progress. Then make adjustments. When you make a guess and then compare results, you will steadily improve your skill in planning and your efficiency in advertising. Comparing plans to actual results is critical. It should be an ongoing practice of every professional Bootstrap Entrepreneur.

· · · · · · · · · · ·

*If you can't measure it, you can't
manage it!*

· · · · · · · · · · ·

Plan your advertising. Start with a budget. Here is a formula I have used with many different businesses. The answer you get is not absolute, but it's an excellent first step.

Advertising Budget Guideline

Projected
new sales $_____ × 15%   = $_____

Existing
sales $_____ × 5%   = $_____

Total
sales $_____ Advertising $_____

The key is to project new sales growth you want to add next year. The formula works with a new or existing business. Multiply projected growth in sales by 15 percent. Then multiply current sales by 5 percent. The total of these two will provide a guideline for your new advertising budget. If the business is new, all the sales are new sales. Try it; you'll like it.

Chapter 45

Financial Planning

Whether you are checking out a business to choose or are planning money needs for a business, the financial planning exercise can be a practical guide. In a way, it's a simple commonsense exercise. Yet, the many variables and unknowns can be intimidating.

Start by relaxing. Don't worry about perfection. Give it your best shot and then revise as you think of things you forgot. The only thing for sure—don't bank on any estimate as being certain to come about. It never does. I have a rule of thumb: work out the best financial forecast you can, then double the expenses and cut the sales in half. If you can survive this worst-case scenario, chances are, you have a handle on things.

I've included a simplified Financial Planning Work Sheet. Use it to ask questions of someone who already has a business like the one you contemplate. If you have no one to consult, make your own best guess and review it with your accountant or business advisor. Make several copies so you can test different combinations of sales levels and expenses.

Caution: The suggested list is simplified and does not allow for extensive construction, fixturing, and delays before getting started. If the business you're considering is that complex, you should already have the experience to work out these estimates, or you should get professional help in a hurry!

. . . .

Gross Profit Formula

Sales
– Cost of goods*
= Gross profit

. . . .

---

* Cost of goods is the cost of products you sell, plus freight, installation, and other direct costs, but does not include any overhead expense.

Three Ways to Increase Net Profit

Increase sales

Increase gross profit

- Often *better* than increasing sales
- Usually best for immediate net profit improvement

Reduce expenses

- Contract out employee services
- Reduce overhead costs
- Avoid advertising cuts

Financial Planning Work Sheet

Note: Month 1 is the month you first spend money. Sales may not start until two or three months later.

Month:	1	2	3	4	5	6
Income						
Sales	____	____	____	____	____	____
Cost of goods	(___)	(___)	(___)	(___)	(___)	(___)
Gross profit (Money available)	____	____	____	____	____	____
Expenses						
Advertising	____	____	____	____	____	____
Employees	____	____	____	____	____	____
Rent	____	____	____	____	____	____
Vehicle	____	____	____	____	____	____
Travel	____	____	____	____	____	____
Accounting/legal	____	____	____	____	____	____
Insurance	____	____	____	____	____	____
Tax	____	____	____	____	____	____
Miscellaneous	____	____	____	____	____	____
Other _____	____	____	____	____	____	____
_____	____	____	____	____	____	____
Total expenses	____	____	____	____	____	____
Capital investment (One-time costs)						
Equipment	____	____	____	____	____	____
Fixtures	____	____	____	____	____	____
Remodeling	____	____	____	____	____	____
Deposits	____	____	____	____	____	____
Consultants	____	____	____	____	____	____
Other _____	____	____	____	____	____	____
_____	____	____	____	____	____	____
Total capital	____	____	____	____	____	____
Monthly money needs*	____	____	____	____	____	____
Cumulative need	____	____	____	____	____	____

Note: Personal salary is not included and will require additional cash if a salary is required.

*Gross profit minus expenses and capital costs.

Net Profit Formula

$$Sales$$

$$- \underline{Cost\ of\ goods}$$

$$= Gross\ profit$$

$$- \underline{Operating\ expenses}$$

$$= Net\ profit$$

(Subtract cost of goods from sales, and you have gross profit. Subtract operating expenses from gross profit, and the remainder is net profit. Do not include any loan payment or salary/draw for yourself as an operating expense.)

Part 7

Get Set

Chapter 46

Incorporate— Yes or No?

Your business can take three legal forms. The first, a sole proprietorship, is a legal extension of the owner of the business. The second is a corporation. The third is a partnership. Your lawyer may recommend that you incorporate. He or she will caution you about the risk of liability in excess of your insurance. Your lawyer will explain that even if your corporation fails, you may personally escape bankruptcy or financial devastation.

This advice is not wrong, and you should consider it. But you must also balance it against business risk and realities. Sometimes the safest course is also a costly course. Balancing risk against cost is a business judgment. The Bootstrap Entrepreneur will be called on to make such judgments daily.

The cost of incorporation may be from $300 or $400 to more than $2,000, depending on the state where you live and legal fees in your area. Also, accounting costs and taxes may be affected. Consider postponing incorporation in the early stages of operation. Why?

First, be certain you have adequate personal liability insurance for your business. Discuss this subject with your agent. The cost is modest. Yes, there is a chance that a legal judgment may exceed your insurance. But it is unlikely.

Second, your corporation will not protect you personally from business debts in the beginning. No businesslike creditor will permit you to purchase on an open account without your personal guarantee. Therefore, hiding from debt behind a corporate shield just doesn't work for a new business.

Almost three out of four businesses in America are sole proprietorships. If you take the risk not to incorporate in the beginning, you will be joining the company of more than 10 million others who did the same.

Important! I do not practice law. You should discuss these issues with your lawyer and accountant and reach your own conclusions.

Chapter 47

Why You Think You Want a Partner, but You Really Don't

Men and women who start a business often want a good friend or career associate to join them in the new venture. At first glance, a lot seems to be going for this idea. One person may complement the strengths of the other. In many examples of partnerships in American business, an outside salesperson teams up with an inside financial person. Or a research scientist teams up with a marketing expert and also a venture capitalist.

When you're a new business owner, sharing victories and setbacks with someone you know is reassuring. You have someone with you, someone on your side. Even better, if one person feels down, the other can give encouragement. Having a partner can offer benefits, and sometimes it is the right thing to do. But generally, for the Bootstrap Entrepreneur, the economics don't shake out.

During the first year of a new business, there is usually not enough revenue to support two families. And there are not enough customers to keep two owner-level individuals busy full-time. Consider the following common partnership scenarios. Two of them don't make sense, and one doesn't work. Let's see why.

Scenario 1: Both partners do inside work. Someone else finds the customers. This approach is ridiculous. Finding customers is the only real job for a new business.

. . . .

Partnerships Don't Work

One partner is generally more talented and productive. She will hold herself back to avoid embarrassing the other. After the partnership breaks up, the productive one may triple the business.

. . . .

Scenario 2: One partner works inside. One partner works outside. This arrangement makes sense on the surface. The problem is, there generally will not be enough customers to keep an inside person busy. The person planning to work inside would do better to get a job and create income. Then this person can take care of bookkeeping and secretarial tasks in the evenings and on weekends.

Scenario 3: Both partners work outside in sales. Each does bookkeeping and secretarial work part-time, or they hire someone to help in these areas. Sounds logical, but here is a fascinating downside. I have seen it happen time and again: One partner will be stronger in sales than the other partner. That's logical. But guess what? The stronger salesperson will not want to embarrass the weaker one. Therefore, the stronger salesperson will hold back while encouraging the weaker partner.

Eventually, these partnerships split up, and what do you think happens? You guessed it! The stronger salesperson continues the business alone and achieves higher sales and much higher profits.

When a Partnership Works

When is a partnership a good thing? It's terrific if two people are going into a business mainly as an avocation. If neither partner needs income for a year or two, then by all means have fun together. Down the road the business may build into something worthwhile.

Another possibility that makes financial sense is when two individuals are experienced in the same industry. They know the business well. Their plans are to have a big business in a short period of time (minimum $200,000 in sales the first year). Ultimately, such a business may build a sales volume of $500,000 to $1 million or even more. This is an excellent use of a partnership in a small business. Other than these two exceptions, be cautious about partnerships.

Chapter 48

Part-Time vs. Full-Time

Working part-time can be a great way to start a new business. Keep your job and your income as long as you can while you organize your business. (See 56, "Getting Organized.")

You may even keep working the first year while building your business. Read more ideas in part 8, "Secrets of Starting on a Shoestring."

Chapter 49

Start Lean and Friendly

Delay a Lease

Wherever possible, let your friendly personality and positive attitude be substitutes for spending money. For example, when some people start a new business, they expect to interview prospects. To do so, they may secure an expensive office in a high-rent district.

On the other hand, the Bootstrap Entrepreneur will find ways to meet prospective buyers in a coffee shop, a hotel lobby, or other low-cost alternative. Through enthusiasm for the business, visual aids in a notebook, and creative ideas, the Bootstrap Entrepreneur may achieve the same sales level without all the expensive trappings.

If an office is essential, hire one on a part-time basis. Try a nearby executive office service company. HQ Company is a nationwide organization. Many similar high-quality independents serve each metropolitan area. Also, check real estate and insurance offices and others that may have extra space available. Avoid long-term lease commitments if you possibly can.

Avoid Inventory

Avoid inventory as long as you can. Order minimum quantities, even at higher prices if necessary. Until the business is established, you are never sure what you will need. Quantity discounts may be appealing. However, you make a wiser move by lowering your investment in inventory and reducing the amount of space you need to store it. As an extreme example, buying a seldom-used product from a competitor at retail may be less costly than keeping it in stock. Even occasionally selling something at cost may be better than storing useless excess.

Use Contract Labor

Hiring employees is another area to hold off as long as you can. Use independent contractors and outside services. Many entrepreneurs provide bookkeeping and accounting services out of their homes. For example, I rely on an excellent typist who works in her home with her own computer, laser printer, and fax and copy machines. She picks up and delivers and provides exceptional service. It's great for her to run a business and care for a new baby. Everyone wins.

Working with a contract person is less costly than hiring a full-time person in your office when there may not be full-time work. By investing in a fax machine, you can have instant communication with typing, bookkeeping, and accounting services outside your business office. If you are computer proficient, you may transmit data by this means as well.

Never hire on-premise employee installers, cleaning services, or fabrication services of any kind. Contract out every function you can, even your salespeople. Salespeople should always work on a commission. You may think it can't be done in your business, but chances are, you can make it work with a little creativity.

As a Bootstrap Entrepreneur, you may not learn all the

solutions in your first year in business, but you need to know the goal you are shooting for. Then you can strive to learn what you need as early as possible.

If You Can't Contract

What if you have no choice? Perhaps you require a retail store, inventory, or employees to start your business. In that event let's get some extra ideas for each of these points.

Chapter 50

Location

What are the reasons you might need a location? One might be for warehouse space to store products, supplies, or equipment. Another might be for office space for you and your employees to work. Another might be for retail or restaurant space for customers to patronize your business. Obviously, your customers are the most important consideration for any space requirement. If the location is not for customers, its whereabouts in the city or its overall appearance doesn't matter much. Obviously, you want a clean, safe environment, but otherwise, you should keep cost to a minimum.

Here are some basic points to remember when securing a location. First, get the best value to achieve your goals, which does not necessarily mean the cheapest rent. If the location is low in cost but fails to achieve your goals, you may have to spend a great deal more to make a change later.

Second, keep your lease commitment to the shortest time possible. If things don't go well your first year, don't be in a position of being obligated to pay thousands of dollars in rent over years to come. (Finding someone to sublease your unneeded space sounds easy, but it isn't.)

You can do this several ways. One way is to take a single-year lease with a two- or three-year option. Your rent cost may be higher by taking only one year, but reducing risk may be worth it. Another way is to negotiate lower rent on a three-year lease but require an escape clause after twelve to eighteen months. If you should need larger or smaller space or none at all at that time, you can give the landlord three to six months' notice to cancel your lease. You may be obligated to pay a fee equal to ninety days' rent or some such amount. But the point is, you have an escape hatch.

A sound idea is to hook up with a major commercial developer who has several properties in your area. That way you can take a smaller space than you think you need. Eventually, when you outgrow it, the developer will be glad to have you move to larger space for the balance of your lease. On the other hand, if you work with a small developer, you will be locked into property that may be too big in the beginning and too small later on.

Chapter 51

Suppliers
and
Inventory

If you must have an inventory of products for resale, try to secure delayed billing from your suppliers for the initial shipment. A good rule of thumb is to ask for three times the normal billing period and settle for twice. For example, if your normal term would be thirty days, try to get ninety-day delayed billing on your first shipment.

If it takes time to assemble or fabricate the inventory you need, try to time your products' arrival precisely with the date of your opening. To help assure this, you can ask your suppliers to "bill and hold." Ask them to keep items in their warehouses until the day you really need them in your store. And of course, try to get the billing date held off as long as possible.

Since you're new to the business, try to negotiate an exchange right in advance. In other words, if some products don't sell, ask for an option to exchange them for faster selling items. When it comes to figuring out exactly what items to carry in inventory—whether it's paint, dresses, gift items, or whatever—sometimes it may be wise not to be too smart.

Sharpie entrepreneurs who know all the answers will make their own decisions about which products to buy and then eat their mistakes later on.

Instead, ask each supplier's employees to use their best experience to give you the fastest turning products possible. Give the supplier a budget, say $5,000, that you are willing to invest in its line. Then discuss your order with your sales representative and a corporate executive. Let both know you are putting yourself in their hands. You are relying on their excellent judgment. Chances are, if they make a mistake on some items, they will be more willing to make an exchange than if you had selected the merchandise on your own.

Chapter 52

Employees

If you must hire employees in the early stage of your business, consider starting them part-time. Interview with the idea of flexibility in their working hours. Also, never just "hire" people. Instead, recruit them to be a vital part of the future of your great enterprise. Don't accept people who are worth only the wage you offer. Find people who are worth more, and who ultimately will earn more, but are willing to take less money at first. Ask them to work side by side with you and to grow with you as your business grows.

These employees will be more valuable. They will bring you customers and keep the ones you have—much more so than people who just want a job. These employees are not hired for money. They are attracted magnetically to Boot-strap Entrepreneurs who have a dream for the future and know how to make it real.

When you attract trustworthy and talented people, be sure you treat them as such. Give them authority and responsibility. Give them a key to the premises. Treat them with openness and trust. You will be rewarded with loyal people who will benefit your customers and your business.

. . . .

*Educate and empower employees,
customers, suppliers, and everyone
you meet.*

. . . .

Chapter 53

Finding
Money

As a Bootstrap Entrepreneur, you may believe that finding money is the most essential decision for your new business. It is not. If you truly need it, you will find it. There are ways to find money, and there are ways to reduce the need for money. We will discuss some of them in part 8, "Secrets of Starting on a Shoestring." If you don't have much money, you join good company. A study of one hundred companies on the 1989 *Inc.* magazine's list of the five hundred fastest growing private companies in the United States indicated:

. . . .

More than 80% . . . were financed through the founder's personal savings, credit cards, second mortgages, and in one case, "a $50 check that bounced."
—Amar Bhide, assistant professor of general management
Harvard Business Review

. . . .

For now, let's review some other points about money. Books in the library suggest all kinds of ideas. Government agencies are set up to help new entrepreneurs, especially women and minorities. Some banks have friendly attitudes toward potential business owners. Every metropolitan Sunday paper will have a classified section with individuals offering money to loan. Venture capitalists look for promising new businesses to loan money to.

Pursuing most of these avenues is a waste of time for the Bootstrap Entrepreneur. Why? These resources want to lend more money than you need. Half of Bootstrap Entrepreneurs start a new business for less than $20,000. Three out of four invest less than $50,000. That means your capital needs are probably modest. Let's assume you need $10,000 to $30,000. If you really want your own business, you probably have adequate resources:

- Some savings, say $5,000 to $10,000
- A good credit rating
- Equity in a home
- At least one automobile with equity value
- Parents, relatives, or loved ones who believe in you enough to help you start your new venture
- A banker who will loan you money on your collateral and on your signature
- Suppliers who believe in you and will help finance your initial purchase
- A franchisor who believes in you and will help finance part of your franchise investment

Only a few Bootstrap Entrepreneurs have all the money sources on this list. Fortunately, it is not necessary to have them all. Two or three are probably sufficient. The financial cornerstone for many entrepreneurs in America today is the equity value in their homes. One of the best types of loans is a revolving line of credit that allows you to pay interest only, if you choose. Then you can pay down the principal when you're in a position to do so.

In other words, you don't need fancy Small Business Administration financing or sophisticated venture capitalists to help you get started. You already have the resources. Use them.

Chapter 54

Too Much Money Is Worse Than Not Enough

When you open your business bank account, be careful. Keep the minimum sensible amount of money you can in your account. Estimate your expenses and cash flow for the first sixty to ninety days. Provide for them properly but no more.

I have seen too many new business owners listen to bad advice. They are told to have plenty of working capital. The result? The bank account looks great for several months. Then, suddenly, things turn rotten overnight. Why?

There is something corrupting about having money in the bank. It allows us to sleep easily and to avoid stress. It helps us put off till tomorrow what we should be doing today. It fogs our thinking and prevents us from realizing the critical urgency to get out and create income at once. Stress and tension can be good if they wake us up to do the right thing.

Yes, you may want some strategic reserves—perhaps capacity to draw down on your line of credit or additional stocks and bonds you can sell in an emergency. But try hard to live on what you have without digging deeper into your savings or your credit line.

This point is one of the most fundamental you can learn about finances. Don't, please don't, think it does not apply to you. It does.

Chapter 55

Housekeeping Chores

One of the last things you will do is to take care of all the nettlesome and annoying housekeeping chores, which include all the legal, tax, and other compliance matters every business owner has to deal with. Until you get into your business, you won't believe all the red tape, paperwork, and pain-in-the-neck stuff a Bootstrap Entrepreneur has to put up with.

Never, never, quit your job until you complete these things. Some will take days and even weeks. Yet, you may not be able to begin selling until you finish them. Do them on your lunch hour or on a vacation day, but don't quit your job.

Here's a partial list of chores to finish before you leave your job:

1. Have stationery, letterheads, envelopes, and business cards printed. Keep them simple; use stock, not custom, logos. Select white or light-colored paper with matching low-cost envelopes. Choose simple single-

panel business cards. Order small quantities of every-thing. A hundred is enough to start, except business cards. Using a good quality photocopy machine might look almost as good as printing and save you money.

2. Get a sales tax number. Look in the phone book under state offices, or dial 411 and ask for help.

3. Get business licenses—from your city, county, and maybe the state. Your accountant probably knows the ones you need. I can't recommend it, but I have seen some Bootstrap Entrepreneurs just go into business until the government tells them what to do. Then they comply right away.

4. Your accountant will help you with a federal tax iden-tification number and FICA filings. Don't fuss with the feds. Whatever they say, do.

For more ideas, visit your library. Two excellent books for technical, legal, and accounting issues are listed in the Bibli-ography. Call your nearest U.S. Small Business Administra-tion Office. A representative will offer ideas without charge. Your accountant or CPA will also have many answers. Avoid asking your lawyer anything except the most critical ques-tions unless the phone call is free. Your lawyer's rate will be the most expensive advice you're likely to pay for.

Chapter 56

Getting Organized

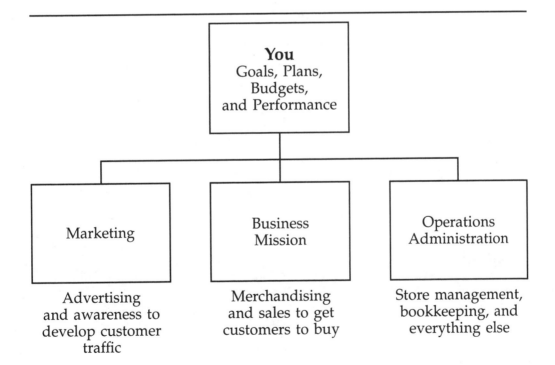

You
Goals, Plans, Budgets, and Performance

Marketing	Business Mission	Operations Administration
Advertising and awareness to develop customer traffic	Merchandising and sales to get customers to buy	Store management, bookkeeping, and everything else

These functional departments exist for every business, no matter how small. Bigger business may have more departments or divide some of them into separate multiple departments. Marketing may be divided into advertising as one department and public relations as a separate department, for example. Another example is operations. A print shop may require a press person, a counter person, and a bookkeeper.

It's important to think of these as separate departments because soon you may have separate people in each one reporting to you.

Begin at once to think about the different jobs you're doing and how you will replace yourself in one department after another.

That's how you get "promoted." You hire someone to take your place, then you concentrate on higher priorities and decision making.

Part 8

Secrets of Starting on a Shoestring

Chapter 57

Secrets of Shoestringing

Starting on a shoestring is a form of guerilla warfare. Shoestring strategies blast away mountain-size obstacles with nickels and dimes.

It's a way of thinking that sophisticated businesspersons would laugh at. They would tell you, "Forget it." They would probably also tell you to go back to your job until you've saved enough money to get into business the "right" way.

So, you should know up front that this advice is not for everybody. It's for the person who has more desire than capital, more drive than patience. The secret principle boils down to this:

. . . .

Create customers before you
spend money!

. . . .

That's it. That's the whole idea. In this part, I will relate real-life examples of how others have done it. Your creative imagination can adapt these ideas to work in your business.

If you don't have to use shoestring strategies, that's great. If you want to use some of the ideas but not all of them, that's fine, too. The point of the exercise is to give you, the Bootstrap Entrepreneur, the option to start your business in a conventional mode with all the cost-saving ideas you've seen so far or to go to the outer edge of bizarre Bootstrap business behavior—to take added risk and face a greater challenge to start on a shoestring. Here's how!

Chapter 58

Shoestringing
Part-Time

If you don't have money to invest, you probably won't have enough money to live month to month without a job. That's okay. Keep your job. Every dollar you earn from your job equals many dollars in sales you won't have to make. But can starting a new business on a part-time basis really work?

I touched on this idea in an earlier chapter. Now, let's dig deeper. I've seen dozens of people start a business while holding a full-time job. And some of those Bootstrap Entrepreneurs who worked part-time in their new businesses actually achieved higher sales than other owners who supposedly devoted full-time to their businesses. Why?

The answer is found in the old adage, "If you have an important project, give it to a busy person." People who are busy seem to develop a rhythm. Any person who has made a list of ten things she thought could never be done in a single day, and then completed the entire list by 11:00 A.M., understands this concept.

. . . .

Work expands to fit the time allowed.

. . . .

Some jobs are well suited to allow time to start a new business. Nurses can work evenings and start a new business in the daytime. As hardworking professionals, many succeed this way, especially if they sell products that doctors and other medical professionals might use. Airline crew members have many nonflying days to start a new business. The same is true of teachers; with the summer and holidays off, teachers who have ambition have the opportunity.

Fire fighters with a work schedule of twenty-four hours on and twenty-four hours off are well positioned to build a good business on the side. Law enforcement officers can adjust their shift schedules to start a business. If these opportunities don't fit your work schedule, consider finding a job that will, for example, night auditor at a hotel or maybe security officer. Ideally, it should be a job where you can do paperwork for your new business while properly performing duties for your employer.

Or the business you choose could target evening customers you can meet after your daytime hours. Many entrepreneurs begin a sales interview at 9:00 P.M. and finish after midnight. So what? That's how Bootstrap Entrepreneurs build a business.

Chapter 59

Shoestringing Productive Time

The most successful entrepreneurs are those who spend more than sixty hours but less than seventy hours a week in their businesses. That's about twelve hours a day. That does not mean every hour of every day must be spent in a store waiting on customers. It might mean opening mail or doing routine paperwork in front of the TV in the evening. It might mean getting up an hour earlier each morning to pay bills or working later in the evening to keep appointments with customers. It also might mean skipping lunch to serve clients. That's being productive.

The reality is this: a motivated business owner should be twice as effective as a new employee. And that same owner who puts in a twelve-hour day works 50 percent more than other employees. If you are twice as effective and work 50 percent longer, you are equivalent to three full-time employees! Try working twelve hours a day. It's fun.

You don't have to sacrifice quality family time to work twelve hours a day. I was missing out on getting to know my new baby son by working until eight o'clock every night.

Eric was put down to sleep just as I came home. Then I realized 8:00 A.M. to 8:00 P.M. is twelve hours, but so is 6:00 A.M. to 6:00 P.M. Try leaving for work at 5:30 A.M. There are less traffic and a nicer group of people.

Organize Around Customers

When working outside calls, I learned to organize time around my customers. Selling drapery fabrics to retailers, I found different stores had different hours. Dry cleaners and paint stores opened their doors at 7:00 A.M. Carpet stores followed at 8:00 A.M. Furniture and department stores opened between 9:00 and 10:00 A.M. Decorating studios opened by 11:00 A.M. At lunchtime people were hard to find, so I traveled between 12:00 and 1:00.

If a customer had not returned from lunch, I caught up on doing paperwork or reading. After 5:00 P.M., stores began to close, except the dry cleaner who stayed open till 7:00 P.M. And furniture and fabric stores in shopping centers stayed open until 9:00 P.M. The owners or buyers were not always in at the late hours, but sometimes they were.

Owners Work Evenings

Then I discovered something about small store owners. Many preferred to work in the evening. They wanted to spend daylight hours selling to customers. Many times I could get an appointment at 8:00, 9:00, or even 10:00 P.M. On more than one occasion the sale was concluded after midnight.

The point is, use your time productively to see customers when they are available. Save reading, doing paperwork, opening mail, bookkeeping, ordering, and working on things like that for late evening or early morning, times when you can't see customers.

Chapter 60

Shoestringing an Office

As a Bootstrap Entrepreneur starting on a shoestring, you can be more creative than to pay rent for an office. One easy answer is to work from home. I started that way in 1970, but in a small apartment with a crying baby, it didn't last long. Then I discovered another idea—and it can work for you. I "moved" to a nearby coffee shop, the kind you can find anywhere. Taking a portable file full of paperwork, I arrived at 7:00 A.M. in time to get my favorite booth and favorite waitress.

I started to work immediately while enjoying a light breakfast. When I was finished, I didn't have to put things away in the refrigerator or clean the table as I did at home. Coffee was brought as fast as I could drink it. It was a great place to work! I often stayed until after 3:00 P.M. A pay phone nearby was perfect to call customers from, and the answering service could reach me if necessary. If I was out, my waitress took the call. She was great and more than earned the extra tip I always left.

Distractions from gabby customers and clattering dishes

bothered me at first, but I learned to concentrate in noisy surroundings. (It's easier today with walk-around stereos and earphones to shut out noise.) I operated that way for a year and a half to save $60 a month. To this day, I do some of my most productive work in coffee shops.

Prospect Interviews

What about interviews with prospects? A coffee shop is all right for many interviews. But what about your best customers? Use a first-class hotel lobby or restaurant. As recently as 1987, after moving to California, I began building a sales organization by interviewing at the La Jolla Marriott Hotel. It's a first-class way to meet people. It was often convenient for them, and it worked fine for me.

Remember, it's not the surroundings; it's the attitude that counts. Many people believe they need a fancy decorated office to sell franchises with a $25,000 investment. Yet, I conducted the first two of a record-breaking forty franchise sales that year in a junky atmosphere—an open-span warehouse with concrete floors and no heat. We had to wear coats, even in San Diego. Keep in mind, our net worth was substantial at that point in my business career. But I operated as if every dime was precious. It was. It still is.

Chapter 61

Shoestringing Furniture and Equipment

If you must have furniture and equipment for your new shoestring venture, buy it used and refurbish it. It's surprising what a little paint will do. Or use Con-Tact paper. That's how I covered a file cabinet burned and scarred in a fire. And I put it in a corner so only two sides had to be covered. The other two were hidden by walls.

Check your Sunday paper. You will be astonished at the variety of used desks, chairs, typewriters, computers, adding machines, fax machines, answering machines, telephone systems, and everything else you need. Yes, you take a risk that some items won't work. Yes, it helps if you know something about the equipment so you can evaluate the risk. But my experience has been very good. If the thing worked when I looked at it, it usually worked when I brought it back to the business. (I bought a used back-up computer to type the manuscript for this book. It's slow, but it works.)

After buying all the copy machines, fax machines, and other equipment I needed, I called in a local repair service and bought a maintenance contract for $50 a month. It didn't make any difference whether it was new or used equipment. The price was the same. So, for a few hundred dollars a year I had to budget anyway, I was able to save thousands of dollars on used equipment. The same was true with steel shelving and equipment for the warehouse.

Whether you need a forklift, a truck, store fixtures, or anything else, buy it used and save 60 to 80 percent off the new cost.

Chapter 62

Shoestringing Rooms for Meetings, Conferences, and Training Events

While uptown entrepreneurs are going broke in posh of-fices and fancy conference rooms they rarely use, you, the Bootstrap Entrepreneur starting on a shoestring, can always find a place to meet for free. Of course, there are obvious solutions, such as a quiet corner in a restaurant where four to six people can meet for a one- or two-hour conference. But sometimes you need more than that. Here are some ideas to think about.

Most people eat breakfast or lunch. Why not have your meeting in a closed-off room provided by the restaurant? Let people chip in for their share of the meal, and your meeting room is free.

For a group of up to a dozen or so, many banks have a conference room they will allow customers to use. What could be more classy than meeting in a bank?

Most shopping centers have a community room. If your meeting is not overtly commercial, they may let you use it at no cost (they like your attendees to visit the mall). Other possibilities include libraries, churches, and maybe even a city or government agency. What about suppliers? Perhaps they have showrooms or training rooms for their sales staff.

Someone's home can be a super place to hold a meeting. It's pleasant, intimate, and productive. Or what about someone's office after hours or on weekends? Then copy machines and other equipment are handy if you need them. The possibilities are endless for the creative Shoestringer.

Chapter 63

Shoestringing Accounts Receivable

Shoestringing and *accounts receivable* are an impossible contradiction of terms. Having an entry for accounts receivable in your books means someone owes you money because you sold on credit. No Bootstrap Entrepreneur, especially not one starting on a shoestring, should ever, ever, ever, ever, sell on credit.

This caution is especially true if you sell to other independent businesses. Business owners are notoriously poor credit risks. Intelligent small business owners want to pay cash so they don't bury themselves in debt.

Small business owners who don't ask to pay cash are often put on COD anyway by their suppliers. Suppliers know they are doing these businesses a favor. It simplifies bookkeeping and assures they can stay in business. So, don't fight the system, Shoestringer. Don't give credit.

Yes, yes, yes. I know this advice is in direct contradiction to what you were told about *getting* credit from your supplier to start your business. But at the beginning of the book, I told you there would be days like this. I said you would be faced with business issues where principles clash. This is one of those days. Use common sense and judgment to solve this conflict the best way you can.

Anyway, the subject is your giving credit to other people, not your getting it from other people. When do you give credit? Never, never, never, never, never, never, never, never, never, never.

Chapter 64

Shoestringing Product Inventory

I hate inventory. The only thing I hate worse is accounts receivable. But you know that by now. Creative thinking can substitute for buying product inventory. Obviously, if you need a retail store for people to look at, buy, and take out products, you're going to need some inventory. But if there's any way to sell from samples or catalogs or displays or anything else that will reduce inventory, for goodness sakes, do it. Here are two interesting stories about products and inventory. Perhaps you'll get a creative idea from one.

Biodegradable Bags

A friend is a top executive at a world-famous chemical company. He told a story about how the company developed a biodegradable garbage bag. The investment in research, testing, production, packaging, and distribution just for test markets cost in excess of $1 million.

Unfortunately, that was in the early 1980s before consumers were so conscious about the environment. Result: the bags didn't sell. The whole project was a flop. My friend explained that although such a large and ethical company could never do such a thing, it would have been far cheaper to use a different approach.

If they had put the same old product into a package printed *biodegradable,* they could have hired a full-time person at each store to stop every customer who purchased a package. They could have given the customer $20 and said, "Sorry, this is a test. We just wanted to see if people would actually buy this stuff."

Moral of the story: find a way to see if the public accepts your product before you manufacture and before you put it into inventory. Even if it seems that it costs a lot more for small quantities, it may cost a lot less than throwing away a bunch of stuff that doesn't sell.

Sell It Before You Own It

With a partner, I started a fabric distributing company in the 1960s. We went to New York to select $10,000 in decorative fabrics—about 150 bolts of different styles and colors. It was going to take sixty days for them to make up sample swatches and send the product to us. Then we would need to send the samples to retailers and wait for their orders. But what could we do for the next ninety days until orders started arriving? We had to survive, and no money was coming in. The supplier had a great idea. Why not cut off yard-length swatches of the top fifty styles and take them on the road to sell advance orders?

That's exactly what we did, selling $2,000 a week in bolts to drapery shops and decorators. We told the customers to expect delivery in a few weeks. We saw several hundred potential customers in the next sixty days. We created awareness about our new company and asked customers for their business. We got the word out person-to-person and at the same time sold enough product to cover our travel expenses and build up a pool of orders.

By the time the inventory arrived, it was almost sold out. Our business was off and running, making a profit in less than ninety days—a feat almost unheard of in a wholesale business. How can you use this idea in your business?

Chapter 65

Shoestringing on Your Competitor's Inventory

A few years later, our wholesale business experienced a devastating fire. We wanted to keep our customer base and not let them buy from someone else. We came up with a great idea. We approached a competitor who handled many of the same product lines we sold. We arranged for our competitor to serve our customers from his inventory! It worked perfectly. We shared the gross profit. Our business retained two-thirds, and our competitor kept one-third.

The real surprise was, we could have operated that way in the very beginning. We could have had a smaller warehouse and smaller inventory and much lower overhead costs.

Could this shoestring idea work for you? Do you have a competitor, maybe just outside your primary market, who would ship for you and give you two-thirds of the profit?

Chapter 66

Shoestringing on a Competitor's Equipment

Perhaps you're starting a business that requires a special machine or costly piece of equipment. Maybe it's a large truck to make deliveries or a special printing press or something that appears necessary but may not be.

Why not go to a competitor who has similar equipment but excess capacity? Maybe he will let you make most of the profit if you find the customers. An excellent example was a young man in the South who wanted to start a drapery dry cleaning business.

The very finest equipment was made by a manufacturer in Cincinnati. The machine pleated and stretched draperies to their original shape after dry cleaning. The equipment cost nearly $15,000, a lot of money for a new business. The enterprising young man went to a local dry cleaner who already had the machine. He told the competitor he would market and find customers if the competitor would process the orders at a fair price. They agreed, and the young man started immediately.

With a strong promotional program telling customers the

benefit of using the best equipment, the young man built a high volume in a short period of time. Originally, he intended to buy the equipment and have a location of his own. But the business was so profitable for him and his competitor that he continued the arrangement as it was.

Could you adapt this idea to your business? It's amazing how many competitors might appreciate extra business, even at a price so low that you could keep a lot of profit for yourself. As a rule of thumb, if you can keep two-thirds of the gross profit without having a location, plant, equipment, employees, and other overhead costs, you are far better off to do so. Be a marketing organization. Let somebody else handle all the other problems.

Chapter 67

Shoestringing Financing

Frankly, I'm nervous telling you this one. It's a bizarre guerilla tactic, but the idea is creative and has possibilities. Warning! Exercise extreme caution.

Perhaps you've seen those TV shows with real estate promoters telling how to make $1 million without any investment. I saw two or three of those programs. But in a classic segment, the promoter asked the audience if they had good credit. Almost everyone answered, "Yes." He then asked, "Can you qualify for $1,000 on a VISA or MasterCard?" Again, "Yes."

"Fine, there's your answer," he crowed. "Just go out and apply for fifty different credit cards with a $1,000 credit line. Now you have $50,000 in working capital to buy your first home!"

Ridiculous? Maybe. Scary? Yes! But if this idea is used in moderation, it is a possibility. What if only ten cards were applied for, with a total credit line of $10,000? If you are doing things suggested in this book, you may not even need the $10,000. Still, having reserves if you really need them for a valid business purpose is reassuring.

But what about the ridiculous interest rate of about 18 percent per year? Yes, it is outrageous. On the other hand, you're likely to pay 10 percent or so to borrow money anywhere. The difference is about 8 percent. Even if you borrowed a full $10,000 at an 8 percent premium, it would cost only $800 extra over the next year. So, you need to ask yourself, Is it worth an additional $67 per month of tax-deductible expense to start my own business? Of course, that question begs the real one: Can I make the payments at all?

Again, I agree with you, it's a crazy shoestring idea. Even if it was reported by the *Harvard Business Review* as an option used by fast-growing entrepreneurs, I don't endorse it. Still, the option and the choice should be yours.

Part 9

Go!

Chapter 68

Hit the Street Running

Starting your own business will likely be the most exciting project you've ever managed. Alone, you orchestrate every move. From locating suppliers to buying merchandise, from renting space to getting an operating license, from advertising to bookkeeping, you bring all the pieces together.

Pat yourself on the back. Sure, there will be foul-ups, disappointments, setbacks, and maybe challenges you think can never be overcome. They go with the territory and are perfect training to prepare you for bigger and better projects in the future. But you will never forget launching your first business!

Soon you will experience the thrill of your first sale. Many business owners frame their first dollar and save it for a lifetime memory. But most important, your first sale should come promptly. In the final days before launch, and in those golden days just afterward, keep a sense of urgency and movement. Set mental deadlines for all you do. Written ones are even better.

Activities that once took days when you worked for

someone else must now be accomplished in hours. But that's part of your new job as a manager.

. . . .

An effective manager compresses time.

. . . .

Lots of businesses can sell $10,000. But will they sell $10,000 in a year, a month, a week, or a day? It's your job to do it as soon as you can. Keep your mind focused on generating sales. Then hit the street running and never stop.

Chapter 69

Sell Your Dream to Everyone

You have a dream, a big dream. Otherwise, you would not have started your own business. You have a dream about what you want for yourself and your family. And because you are the kind of person you are, you have a dream about what you will contribute to your customers. Tell these dreams to everyone you meet!

Be sure everyone knows what you plan to do for your customers and for your community. Tell your story to the banker, the grocery clerk, the plumber. Tell it to everyone. Be sure they all know who you are and what you're doing. Write your ideas in a pamphlet with your photograph. Include your mission statement. It could be as simple as a single page of your stationery announcing your opening. At the absolute minimum give out your business card. On the front or back, print three or four major customer benefits.

Make a list of everyone on your Christmas card list, everyone you pay bills to, everyone you know in churches and organizations. Be sure all of them know about your dreams and plans. Ask them to tell their friends. Tell them you appreciate their help to get your business started.

When you believe in what you're doing and its benefit to others, your enthusiasm is contagious. Make a photo album with visual ideas about what you do and where you're going. Use copies of your advertising, brochures, news stories and, most of all, photos of satisfied customers using your products. Get their written comments as testimonials. Have maps, charts, and graphs to show your goals. If you sell your dream to everyone, your business is bound to succeed.

Three Ways to Increase Sales

Increase shoppers

- Get more traffic through the door
- Make more appointments in homes or businesses

Increase conversion rate

- Turn shoppers into customers

Increase each sale

- Promote add-ons and extras

Chapter 70

You Are the Business

Every business projects the values and philosophies of its founder or CEO.

Now you have the chance to build a business by your set of values. The way you handle yourself as a business professional will affect every person you touch and your reputation for the rest of your life.

It's not easy being a professional—having the correct, positive attitude at all times, being responsible to arrive at every appointment on time, paying bills on time, following up with customers on time, and so on.

As a Bootstrap Entrepreneur, you have joined a special group of people who stand tall, stand independent, and stand proud. So, remember you *are* the business. Stand special.

Chapter 71

Make a Friend

Some years ago, I had the privilege of meeting an exceptional Bootstrap Entrepreneur in the small town of Hereford, Texas. She was hardworking, innovative, and just as basic and rock solid as the hard dry farmlands around her. On a per-capita basis, Rena Rae Newton built one of the highest volume businesses in her industry in less than three years.

When asked her secret of success, she answered, "Well, whenever I met a customer, I would just try to make a friend. I would listen to her, hear her ideas, and then I just tried to help her out." Rena Rae's make-a-friend philosophy became one of the founding concepts of the most successful interior decorating sales organizations in the world. Truthfully, I think it's the founding philosophy of every great sales organization everywhere, even if it's not expressed with the simple eloquence Rena Rae gave to the world.

It's not enough just to make a friend. It's important to *keep* a friend. When your friend becomes a customer, wouldn't it be nice to send a thank-you note? Possibly even flowers? Maybe tickets to the theater? Do something extra and you'll keep your friends as customers for a lifetime.

Chapter 72

Path
to Profits

I've created a diagram setting out the essential elements of your business and called it Universal Path to Profits.

These elements apply to every Bootstrap Entrepreneur's business. Some big company essentials are left out—manufacturing, research and development, and things of that nature. However, for the vast majority of independent businesses in America, this illustration should be useful.

Whenever profits in your business are not measuring up to your expectations, come back to this diagram. Chances are, the solution is on it. It will identify fundamental issues so you can point yourself in the right direction.

This diagram is easily the subject of a separate book. If you like this book, perhaps I'll write that one later. In the meantime, use this diagram as an outline for your initiative.

Universal
Path to Profits

Awareness
Advertising and promotion cause shoppers to become aware of your name and the products/ services you offer.

Meet Shoppers Face-to-Face
When you are considered an option, shoppers walk into your store or invite you to make a presentation.

Convert Shoppers to Customers
After you meet shoppers, they buy something because of your merchandise or sales skill.

Gross Profit
A sale results in gross profit, which is the difference between what you pay for products/ services and what you sell them for.

Expenses
Expenses are paid from gross profit. Expenses include advertising, salaries, rent, supplies, insurance, and other overhead costs (but not owner's pay).

Net Profit
Net profit results when expenses are less than gross profit. Net profit includes payments on loans; company cars and business equipment used personally; draw, salary commissions, and all other income and benefits received by owner.

If you don't have the net profit you want, the answer is in one of the steps above.

Chapter 73

Pricing
and Profits

If there is any single area you will probably be self-conscious about, it is the retail price you set for your products and services. You will probably be afraid to set them high enough. You may have a defensive feeling that big businesses can buy for a lot less than Bootstrap Entrepreneurs. Oftentimes, that is correct. But low price is not the only reason customers buy.

Look around. In spite of wholesale clubs, discount stores, and other big businesses whose pride is low price, literally millions and millions of small businesses survive, compete, and grow. The fact is, the majority of independent entrepreneurs could raise prices, and revenues would not drop. But our point now is a different one.

As a new Bootstrap Entrepreneur, you should set your prices high enough to be sure you make a profit. Never start with base prices lower than similar competition. Yet, you may want to open a market with temporary promotional values and introductory offers.

If you run a grand opening promotion, offer some products priced near or even at cost. Give customers an exciting value on certain items, and chances are, they will pick up other products at regular price while they're there.

If you're making in-home sales and you're talking to a potential customer you feel can be valuable to your future either to make repeat purchases or to be an opinion leader, think twice before you lose the sale. There is nothing wrong with sometimes offering a special value to "buy your way in" *in the beginning*. Even better than reducing price is giving the client added products. The results are more profits for you and more satisfaction for the customer. And your customer receives better overall value.

Pricing is a critical issue. It requires judgment. One suggestion is to use selective low prices to open the market and gradually increase your profit margins as your reputation is established. You can do research by checking your competitors. Find out what they charge. Then ask customers who bought from competitors what they think about your competitors' pricing.

· · · · · · · · · · ·

As managers we can make two mistakes in pricing: (1) Price too high; (2) Price too low. If you price too high, everybody will tell you. If you price too low, nobody will tell you.

· · · · · · · · · · ·

Chapter 74

Follow
the Money

As a Bootstrap Entrepreneur getting started in a new business, focus on things that create money. Avoid things that waste money. To follow the money, watch several basic areas. Monitor advertising carefully. Be sure it's getting you leads and customers. Simplify your product assortment. Achieve maximum sales from minimum inventory. Promote products that yield the best gross profit. Sometimes high-profit products give customers the best satisfaction, so they return again and again.

To follow the money means to steadily improve your gross profit. To manage your expenses. To plan budgets and profit goals. The only way to increase income and avoid waste is to keep accurate records.

As valuable as is money, so is your time. The best way to organize time is the simplest: Keep a monthly calendar, a weekly schedule of appointments, and a daily list of things to do.

Follow the money! Focus on things that create income, avoid waste, and use time effectively. Then before long, the money will follow you!

Chapter 75

Good
Records

Some Bootstrap Entrepreneurs are in such a rush to run a business, their records are in shambles. At one time, I operated the same way. My philosophy was, "Sell first, and clean up the mess later."

Fundamentally, I still believe this principle, but it should be balanced. Instead of throwing scraps of paper in a bushel basket and dumping it on your accountant's desk, try to do a few simple things. First, keep a calendar in your notebook. Make notes of things about money as they happen, right on your calendar.

Next, list details in your check register. Some business owners are so careful to save paper, they lose the story about what happened. Try the opposite. Paper is cheap, but you can waste hours trying to reconstruct records, and that's expensive.

What other records do you need? Mainly those in advertising, sales, and financial areas.

Advertising and Sales

Since creating customers is the whole purpose of your business, the most critical records for your future will include the following:

- Compare a budget plan for advertising to actual expenses.
- Count store walk-in traffic, or if sales are made outside the store, count appointments.
- Count customers actually sold (whether in store or outside the store).
- Count total sales—daily if you have a store, and weekly and monthly in all cases.

If you capture this information, you can make studies later. Analyze the effectiveness of your newspaper in getting leads. Check your closure rate for sales presentations outside the store or the purchase rate for customers who come to your store. This way you can establish operating standards for your business. You will be able to make month-to-month and year-to-year comparisons. *The first essential to improve anything is to know where you are now. Otherwise, you will never know if you got better or worse.* Remember, *if you can't measure it, you can't manage it!*

Financial Records

If you want to earn profits, financial records are just as important as sales records. Here are some essential ones:

- Record all deposits. The best way is to photocopy every check and deposit slip.
- Keep a clear and complete check register.
- Match up purchase order copies and receiving tickets for every product you buy.
- Use a cost-control ticket for each job if you do custom work of any kind or if you combine multiple products,

services, and supplies for a single customer sale. List the cost of each product, fabrication, installation, and any other items. Your cost-control ticket will help you control and improve gross profit margins on whatever you sell.

. . . .

Next to sales, gross profit is the most important determinant of net profits. (Expenses are easier to manage than gross profit.)

. . . .

- Set up any other records you or your accountant feels are necessary.

Yes, it takes time to keep good records. But without them, you can waste months of unproductive effort. Maintain accurate records in the first place.

Chapter 76

Financial
Statements

The professional Bootstrap Entrepreneur quickly learns the significance of periodic financial statements. Business owners who think they can get by an entire year without a financial statement are foolish. Call them Boneheaded Entrepreneurs.

My best memory about the value of financial statements occurred years ago. I was advising a bright young couple in their early twenties. They had taken over a family carpet business in Middlesboro, Kentucky, and had increased sales about 50 percent during the year. The husband and wife worked extra hard and extremely long hours. Finally, the end of the year rolled around, and the accountant completed their year-end financial statement. When they saw it, they were devastated. In spite of all their hours and efforts, and in spite of increased sales, *their net profit was actually less than the year before!* From that day forward, monthly financials took first priority. Before long, they had an excellent and profitable business.

How often should you get financial statements? As a rule

of thumb, if your business does over $10,000 a month, consider monthly financial statements. Be sure you get them when you cross the $15,000 threshold. If your sales are less than $10,000 per month, quarterly financial statements may be okay. However, you may find it costs only a little extra to get monthly financial statements anyway. Paying only $50 to $100 a month additional may be money well spent. Try monthly at first, then go back to quarterly statements if your business is stable and predictable.

You will be astonished at what you discover each time you receive your financial statement. The more of them you get, and the more you study them, the better you will understand your business. And the better businessperson you will become.

By the way, don't let your accountant use a cash-basis system if you have inventory, accounts receivable, or a delay from the time you take an order until the time you collect the money from your customer. Under these conditions, it is essential that your accounting be on an accrual basis. Your accountant will explain the differences in these two approaches.

Leonard Casey, president of Heritage Custom Kitchens, advised that even more important than a financial statement about what you have done is a financial plan of what you're *going to do.* He put it this way:

. . . .

"Using a financial statement to manage a business is like driving your car by looking in the rearview mirror. It will tell you where you've been, but it won't tell you where you're going."

. . . .

When you develop a good sales and expense plan in advance and then match it against your financial statement, you have the advantage of both. Your financial plan must be measurable and achievable, or it's not a plan at all.

Chapter 77

Who Is the Manager?

You quit your job to start your own business so that *you* could be the boss. What a surprise you are discovering! Now with a few weeks' experience as a Bootstrap Entrepreneur, you probably find instead of one boss you have many—your customers! In addition to customers, sometimes suppliers will be managers when they tell you about a back order or insist on payment for a lost invoice. They assign work for you to do. As a new businessperson, you find your priorities are managed by events you can't control, and by employees, spouse, salespeople, and others who compete for your time. Along with these managers, you will find one more.

The Real CEO!

You, your customers, suppliers, spouse, and employees will soon find yourselves subordinate to the real chief executive officer. Who is this all-powerful entity running your business? *It's your business checkbook!*

Your checkbook is the world's best manager. It will tell

you when you have too much inventory, too much accounts receivable, not enough sales, too many employees, or any of a dozen other things that can go wrong in business. Problems and mistakes always turn up first in your checkbook.

When your checkbook is empty, it's screaming for you to find more customers, collect money from ones who owe you, or cut down on purchases of inventory, supplies, and other things. Conversely, when your checkbook is fat and happy, it's telling you what a wonderful job you're doing as a Bootstrap Entrepreneur.*

You will soon learn it's not smart to ignore your checkbook, no matter who you feel owns the business. If your checkbook CEO could talk, it would have this message: "If you keep me happy, I'll keep you happy."

* Financial experts are correct in saying that cash in the bank may not be a reliable indicator of accrual profits. But for Bootstrap Entrepreneurs in new businesses that do not require sophisticated asset and liability management, it's the best and earliest indicator they have.

Chapter 78

Luck

What does luck have to do with success in a small business? Must a Bootstrap Entrepreneur depend on luck to get ahead? Most owners of a business would deny it. Yet, it is a factor. *New Business in America: The Firms and Their Owners*, an NFIB Foundation report, had this to say about luck in regard to business survival and success: "The element of chance may be more important than many people would like to think."

Other people have had things to say about luck. Dick Gregory, the comedian, once said, "If it wasn't for bad luck, I wouldn't have no luck at all." I've never seen a business fail only because of bad luck, but unpredictable chance does have a bearing on a Bootstrap Entrepreneur's success.

Here are some things I've observed about luck and small business over the years. Without dwelling on the lucky big sale or the unlucky setback that seems to come once or twice every year, let's address the issue of luck on a big-picture, long-term basis.

Entrepreneurs through the ages are famous for being

alert to trends and changes and capitalizing on them. The change may be luck. But knowing how to seize the opportunity is strictly entrepreneurial resourcefulness. Was it luck that the BMW auto people invented "the ultimate driving machine" just as hard-charging, status-conscious yuppies were starting their ascent into the 1980s? If you want to be lucky, watch for change. Then catch the wave and go with it.

. . . .

Here's another thing about luck: it doesn't matter if good luck comes if you went out of business the year before it arrived!

. . . .

Since random chance may bring your business good luck every few years, you must persevere to still be in business when the good luck comes.

Another thing to remember is that one person's bad luck may be good luck for someone else. It was hard luck for all the savings and loan businesses to go belly-up in 1990 and 1991. But what wonderful luck for the well-financed banks and institutions that bought up property at fifty cents on the dollar.

One final thought about luck. Since you can't predict it and you certainly can't control it, you mustn't sit around waiting for it. Instead, stay busy serving your customers. Then you will probably agree with other Bootstrap Entrepreneurs who say, "The harder I work, the luckier I get."

Chapter 79

Lemons
to Lemonade

Now that you know what it takes to start a new business, this final chapter is to help steer you to success. I want to share with you my most valuable lesson learned in thirty years of business. Why does one idea stand taller than all the others? Over the years many setbacks and experiences have taught me valuable lessons. Each contributed in its own way to my business career. But one insight has served so well in so many different circumstances that it stands in a class of its own. On many occasions it resulted in long-term major breakthroughs. This priceless concept can be summarized:

. . . .

Turn your lemons to lemonade.

. . . .

Why is this advice so precious? As a Bootstrap Entrepreneur, you are guaranteed setbacks and temporary failures in your new venture. That's part of owning a business. When you were an employee, you may have been insulated from failure. Your job had a floor—a minimum income to give security. But with a floor also came a ceiling that may have held you back from your full potential. Many employees will never experience the agony of risk and the stress of defeat. And that is sad. Because only by exceeding our limits do we learn where our limits are.

Napoleon Hill may have been the first this century to share such a truth with entrepreneurs. Over fifty years ago, he penned his definitive work, *Think and Grow Rich,* and said,

. . . .

> *"Every adversity, every failure and every heartache carries with it the seed of an equivalent or greater benefit."*

. . . .

As a Bootstrap Entrepreneur, you should know that your character will be strengthened by failure. Your mind will be empowered by experience. When you discover the good, the benefit, and the greater success that come from adversity, you will become a person who has learned to turn lemons to lemonade. This pattern of thinking will carry you forward: over, under, around, and through obstacles. It will help you develop an inner peace and a philosophy that leads to happiness in all you do. Turning lemons to lemonade means discovering your most disastrous setback has within it the opportunity for your greatest success.

A corollary to this principle will prepare you even before you fail. It's an expansion of turning lemons to lemonade.

. . . .

> *Whatever you are most afraid of, brag about it first.*

. . . .

It doesn't matter whether you're afraid that your prices are too high, that your delivery takes too long, that you have too small a store while your competitor has a big store. Whatever you are most afraid of, there is *some* way to brag about it as the strongest selling point of your business. Here are two examples that happened to me some years ago.

Lose the Battle, Win the War

When I was a salesman selling fabric samples to drapery shops and decorators, I prided myself on being tops in sales. Then one season a representative named Henry Tilford began outselling me by a mile. I had over one hundred samples in our new line, and I always sold about half. Back then, that was good enough to be number one every season. But somehow, that season Henry Tilford was leaving me in his dust.

For days I was puzzled and demoralized. But I didn't want to give up. Then one day, as I drove into Ottumwa, Iowa, I had an idea. Why not try to sell one hundred samples at one time—twice my normal amount? To do it, I would have to sell the entire line. But was it possible? I had never done it before, and after three years in the trade, I had never known any salesperson to do such a thing. But I knew if I was going to catch up with Henry, I would have to do something drastic.

On my next call, I sat in the car several minutes to build myself up mentally. Then I went to the door and knocked. The owner, a successful Bootstrap Entrepreneur, greeted me. I asked to show her my sample line. I had never met her before. She knew nothing about me, my company, or our service. It would be a tough sale. But she agreed to look at my line.

I brought in two big black sample cases from the car and began laying out sample after sample. Enthusiastically, I talked up the benefits of every one—the beautiful colors, the excellent design, the attractive pricing. I talked about what a great company I represented and how reliable our delivery was. The more I talked, the more excited I became. But she said hardly a word.

After I presented my last sample, I stood back and said,

"Isn't that a fabulous line of fabrics?" Barely waiting for her nod, I went on, "We are really a terrific company, and I can get you this entire assortment at special savings. There are over one hundred samples. I know your customers will love the fabrics, and you'll do a lot of business. Wouldn't you like to have the *entire line?*"

Dead silence.

Seconds ticked by. I had to bite my tongue not to speak. She looked up slowly, her eyes gazing into mine, and said haltingly, "You know, it is a pretty nice line. I think I'll take it." My hand was shaking so much I could hardly get out an order pad. I wanted to scream and jump up and down and kick up my heels. But I tried to act as nonchalant as my exuberance would permit.

She signed the order, and I packed my cases, gave her a copy, said thank you, and fumbled out the door as quickly as I could without being too obvious. I threw the sample cases in the trunk, jumped in the car, and drove away pounding the steering wheel and screaming at the top of my lungs.

That day, at that moment, I discovered the power of the human mind. From that day forward, I presented the full line every place I went. I didn't always sell every sample, but a surprising thing began to happen. When I asked people to buy the full line, and they said, "No," my follow-up question was simply, "Well, why don't you pick out the three or four you don't like, and I'll write up the rest of them?" *It was fabulous.* They would take away a few samples, and I would write up an order for twice the number I was averaging before.

With my new approach, I didn't take long to catch up to Henry Tilford. But I thank Henry to this day. Had it not been for his causing a setback, I might never have turned lemons to lemonade and discovered the power of mental attitude. That day in Ottumwa, Iowa, was the most important in my career. Because of that success, I developed the confidence and belief that I could start an organization with the dream of having over one thousand franchise operations through-out the country.

Brag About Your Worst Fear

About three years into franchising, I had an idea to expand our product assortment beyond draperies and fabrics. I wanted it to include carpeting, wall covering, and furniture. But there was a real problem. Our decorators already had a trunk full of samples in their cars; there was no room for more. Even those with a station wagon would never find space for fifty wallpaper books plus carpet sample boards and furniture catalogs. The problem nagged at me for days. Our special competitive edge was showing samples in customers' homes, next to their furniture and lighting conditions. If we were to add new products, we had to come up with a new way of thinking, or it would be impossible.

Then at the end of an exhausting week working with franchise owners in North Carolina (talking to customers is one of the best ways to get inspiration), I started home to Indianapolis. It was a lonely ten-hour drive (which is a good way to concentrate). Soon, I began to focus on the problem of too many samples to fit in each decorator's car.

Somewhere north of Knoxville, it came to me that one possible solution would be a truck. No car or station wagon would ever hold the three thousand samples we wanted to carry to our customers. But I knew a truck wouldn't work. Status-conscious interior decorators would never accept their friends calling them truck drivers. I visualized a semitrailer wheeling into a neighborhood with a delicate designer at the wheel. Ridiculous! No way.

So, I kept driving and thinking. It was after 10:00 P.M. I still had five hours to drive. As the car geared up, my mental gears turned. Different thoughts sped through my mind in pace with my speed down the highway. But nothing clicked. Then I remembered the magic words that helped me so many times before when I had an impossible problem: *Turn lemons to lemonade. . . . Whatever you're afraid of, brag about it first.*

But what could I do with this lemon? How could I brag about a truck? I thought and thought. Suddenly, lightning struck. I said to myself, *If we're in a color business, and we want the public to know who we are, why not make the truck a colorful and dramatic traveling billboard? Make it so noticeable, it will get us customers everywhere it goes. And do it with such unique good taste, decorators will be proud to drive it!*

That's it! I said to myself. *That's the answer!* Again I screamed and pounded on the steering wheel. I knew it would work. I even came up with a special name: ColorVan. I began to think how the golden arches are a symbol of McDonald's identity. Then I visualized how the ColorVan would become the symbol of Decorating Den's identity. Did the idea work? Today, interior decorators in over 1,200 ColorVans have served over 500,000 customers in America and in several countries throughout the world.

You Can Do It, Too

You can do the same in your business. Every time you have a setback, ask, How can I turn this lemon into lemonade? Every time you're afraid of something, ask, How can I brag about what I'm afraid of? If you practice this mental skill, you will develop yourself and your wonderful new business to a position of leadership in your community and someday perhaps throughout the world.

With this challenge, I welcome you today as you join a fabulous family of Bootstrap Entrepreneurs everywhere.

Part 10

Looking
Back

Chapter 80

Three Years from Now

Can you visualize what your business will look like three years from now? Look at yourself looking back on the journey you are about to start. What do you feel? What did you learn? What were your experiences? Are you where you wanted to be? Was it worth it? Would you do it again?

If the picture is fuzzy, it's understandable. Without experiencing the experience, it's hard to feel the feeling. But the human mind is so wonderful, it can grasp mental pictures from the experiences of others. Connecting your mind to those of other entrepreneurs who have already experienced three years in business could sharpen your focus.

What Would Experienced Entrepreneurs Say?

Thanks to the NFIB Foundation report *New Business in America: The Firms and Their Owners,* we can call on a unique study of young firms and their progressive experiences over three years. Later, we'll explore ideas from other interviews and experiences.

The NFIB study of almost three thousand independent small business owners revealed valuable insights. First, not every entrepreneur survived. About one out of five discontinued or sold the business. But what did the four out of five who persevered have to say? Their endorsement was telling. Eighty-three percent said they would do it again. About half of them said they would make major changes if they had it to do over. Another 14 percent said they probably would not start exactly the same kind of business once again. But only 3 percent said they were so disillusioned, they would never form another business.

In general, the entrepreneurs had a sense of accomplishment. Many fulfilled their objectives, which motivated them to start a business. Some of the motivations included "use my skills and abilities," "have greater control over my life," "build something for my family," and "[liked] the challenge." In fact, *two out of three reported as much or more personal satisfaction than they expected from the business.*

When it came to money, the majority were not entirely satisfied. They would like to have earned more. When it came to control over their lives, almost two out of three achieved the control they had expected.

Nevertheless, in closing, the authors commented, "After three years of business ownership, enthusiasm appeared tempered by reality . . . but, the vast majority were glad they went into business for themselves and would do so again."

Perhaps learning how other business owners look back on their three years of business experience, you can begin to sense the feeling as if you had been there yourself. The picture emerging seems to say, "Yes, if I had it to do over again, I would change some things. Yes, there were challenges. Yes, there were tough times. Still, I accomplished much of what I set out to do. In some ways, I found more satisfaction than I expected. Bottom line, considering tough times and good, given the choice, I would do it all over again."

Views of Entrepreneurs After Completing Three Years in Business

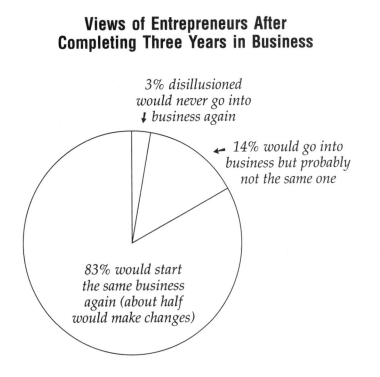

3% disillusioned
would never go into
↓ business again

← 14% would go into
business but probably
not the same one

83% would start
the same business
again (about half
would make changes)

Parallel Experience

This conclusion parallels my observations working with thousands of Bootstrap Entrepreneurs over the years. I asked many of them one question that revealed their true feelings about whether they made the right decision. The question ultimately refined was this:

. . . .

*"How much money would you
require as a salaried employee to
give up your business and go back
to work for someone else?"*

. . . .

Somehow, this question cuts to the quick. Each business owner had to pause and reflect before answering. When I heard the answer the first time, I was surprised. So I asked the question again and again. Each time, I found the pattern the same. As if each was rehearsed by some outside force, I repeatedly heard a similar response.

Not that the amount of salary required was the same; each was different. Some replied $40,000 a year; others, $80,000; others $150,000. The amount of money was not the common denominator. Since I was privy to their financial conditions, I soon realized that without consciously being aware, the people answered *approximately double the earnings in their own businesses!*

Yes, the value the owners subconsciously placed on the freedom of owning a business was roughly double their present earnings and far more than they would likely command as a salary. In their own way, they were telling me and telling themselves, "I wouldn't trade my business for anything."

Now, It's Your Turn

As you become a Bootstrap Entrepreneur, I know the queasy feeling in your stomach, the lump in your throat, the fear your courage must conquer as you face the risk of bringing your dream to reality. But I know you can do it. And I also know that other entrepreneurs who have faced these same fears before you would, if they could, join me in wishing you a prosperous journey and the fondest hope that three years from today you, too, will say, "I wouldn't trade my business for anything."

Good luck, and God bless you.

Appendix 1

Estimated Small Business Start-Ups

Summary	Million
Total U.S. business	18.0
Small business (fewer than 5 employees)	13.5
Total start-ups annually—U.S.	4.0
Small business start-ups with 6 or fewer employees in first year	3.2
Thinking of starting a business	12.8
Total market of persons considering business start-ups or actually starting	16.0

Sources: NFIB Foundation, *Louis Rukeyser's Business Almanac*, and interpretive estimates.

Appendix 2

Selected Facts

Small Business Primer (1988)

	Million	Percent
Types of business organization		
Corporations	3.0	17
Partnerships	1.5	8
Proprietorships	13.5	75
Number of operating U.S. businesses	18.0	100
Farm, nonfarm business; employers and nonemployer-type businesses		
Farm business (Full- and part-time)	2.7	15
Employers (nonfarm)	4.5	25
Employ less than 5 (60% of employers)	2.7	15
Employ less than 20 (90% of employers)	4.05	23
Employ over 50	0.27	1.5
Nonemployers (individual business)	10.8	60
Full-time	3.6	20
Part-time	7.2	40
Total invested capital, prior to first sale		
Group		
I $ 9,000 and less		34
II $ 19,000 and under		49
III $ 10,000 to $ 49,000		40
IV $ 20,000 to $100,000		38
V $100,000 and over		16

Sources: NFIB Foundation Publication, *Small Business Primer* (1988) and *New Business in America* (1990).

New Business in America:
The Firms and Their Owners (1990)

Most important goals when starting business (of the number answering each question, the percentage choosing first or second preference, compared to third, fourth, or no answer)

"Do the kind of work I wanted to do"	49%
"Avoid working for others"	39%
"Make more money than otherwise"	39%
"Build a successful organization"	53%

Importance of selected factors in deciding to go into a business (rated as important or very important)

"Liked the challenge"	73%
"Build something for family"	74%
"Earn lots of money"	46%
"Greater control over my life"	78%
"Use my skills and abilities"	81%

Where did you get the idea to go into this kind of business?

Prior job	43%
Family business	6%
Activities of friendly relatives	6%
Subtotal, business related	55%
Hobby/personal interest	18%
Education/courses	6%
Subtotal, personal interest related	24%
Someone suggested it	8%
Chance happening	10%
No answer	3%

Why did you go into business at the time you did?

Good opportunity came along/I jumped	28%
Considered for a long time; came together	43%
Other reasons	29%

Did your parents ever own a business?   Yes: 45%

Age at which owners start business

20–39	60%
40–49	26%
50 plus	11%

Selected sources of funds to start business

Personal savings provided 20% to 100%	75%
Friends/relatives provided 20% to 100%	25%
Banks provided 20% to 100%	46%

Number of employees, first year

6 or fewer	81%
7 to 10	10%
10 or more	9%

First-year sales

Less than $100,000	33%
$100,000–$199,000	23%
$200,000–$349,000	15%
$350,000–$1,000,000	16%
$1,000,000 and over	7%
No answer	6%

Appendix 3

Interpretive Extrapolations and Experience-Based Estimates

Annual new business start-ups.

The exact number of new sole proprietorship businesses is not a matter of public record (as are corporations), and hard numbers are difficult to find. Based on the historic data from Internal Revenue Service reports, the following is an estimate of total new business start-ups each year.

Assumption: Start-ups are in same proportion as existing business

	Existing	New Annual
Incorporations, minimum 1990s	3.6 million	750,000
Partnerships, 50% Corp.	1.8 million	375,000
Proprietorships, 3.4 x Corp.	12.2 million	2,550,000
Total businesses	17.6 million	3,675,000

Experience validation:

Observation and informal yellow page studies indicate 15% to 20% of 18 million businesses turn over each year .... 2.7–3.6 million

Conclusion:

Minimum number of new business start-ups estimate .... 3.0 million

New business with 6 or fewer employees (NFIB) 81%

Estimated total annual small business start-ups .... 2.4 million

Estimated persons who think/dream of a new business
but take no action—minimum 4 to 1   9.6 million

Total estimated minimum number of people thinking of
or starting a new small business annually   12.0 million

Bibliography

To Prepare You As a Bootstrap Entrepreneur

Carnegie, Dale. *How to Win Friends and Influence People.* This book is the most basic and important one for any business owner.

Hill, Napoleon. *Think and Grow Rich.* Some people are put off by the name. Don't be. This valuable philosophy of life is a distilled outline designed for any person who wants to succeed at any worthwhile endeavor (my personal all-time favorite).

McCullough, Mamie. *I Can. You Can Too!* This book gives you twelve ways to develop a healthy self-image and overcome fear of failure, two ways to successful entrepeneurship.

To Help You Choose a Business

Editors of *Entrepreneur. Entrepreneur Magazine's 111 Businesses You Can Start for Under $10,000.* This source is an excellent listing of businesses that can be started for a low to modest investment.

Entrepreneur. This publication is full of ideas for small business operators and those looking for new business opportunities.

International Franchise Association. *Franchise Opportunities Guide.* This guide lists over two thousand franchising companies and is a super source of information on franchising. The address is 1350 New York Ave., NW, Suite 900, Washington, DC 20005.

Naisbitt, John, and Patricia Aburdene. *Megatrends 2000.* This book examines forces that have been transforming our society and will shape our future.

Popcorn, Faith. *The Popcorn Report.* This book offers insights on trends and opportunities for 1990s and beyond.

To Start a New Venture

Brandt, Steven C. *Entrepreneuring: The Ten Commandments for Building a Growth Company.* From this author, you'll gain ideas that will benefit you in many areas.

Brown, Deaver. *The Entrepreneur's Guide*. This guide offers big business perspectives on people, management, and finance.

Seuss, Dr. *Oh, the Places You'll Go!* This resource is a must read for anyone graduating school, starting a new job, or beginning a business.

To Help You with Marketing and Sales

Bettger, Frank. *How I Raised Myself from Failure to Success in Selling*. You'll learn many beneficial ideas from my single favorite all-time best book on sales.

Hayes, Ira. *Success: Go for It* and *YAK, YAK, YAK*. Ira Hayes is the original ambassador of enthusiasm. He provides simple, usable methods to demonstrate and communicate in a selling situation. I love his ideas and use them myself.

Hopkins, Tom. *How to Master the Art of Selling*. Hopkins has provided an encyclopedia, a college course, on every aspect of sales; the audiocassette program is a bargain at under $200.

Johnson, Spencer, and Larry Wilson. *The One Minute Sales Person*. These two authors have written an excellent fast read to give you the feel and philosophy of successful selling.

Kennedy, Danielle. *Selling! The Danielle Kennedy Way*. Danielle Kennedy is one of the great sales leaders in America. Her book and tapes are great confidence builders and inspirations to women and men everywhere.

Levinson, Jay Conrad. *Guerilla Marketing Attack*. The best book for commonsense, low-cost ways to advertise and find customers will be a worthy addition to your library of business books.

Ziglar, Zig. *Zig Ziglar's Secrets of Closing the Sale*. This work is just one of the many excellent books and audiocassette programs authored by Ziglar. Buy every one you can find. He is one of the best in the business.

To Help You Get Set

Alarid, William, and Gustav Berle. *Free Help from Uncle Sam to Start Your Own Business (or Expand the One You Have)*. This source book explains government assistance for small business—loan programs, information sources, and counseling services.

Jenkins, Michael D. *Starting and Operating a Business in (Your State)*. Loaded with details and specifics of legal, license, tax, and so on, this book will be beneficial in several stages of your business operation.

To Build a Great Business

Drucker, Peter F. *The Effective Executive*. Peter Drucker is perhaps America's most famous management consultant. He has authored dozens of great books. This is one of his earliest and most useful for business owners/ executives.

Townsend, Robert. *Up the Organization: How to Stop the Corporation from Stifling People and Strangling Profits*. One of the all-time great, simple, no-baloney books on business management, it's intended for big business but great if you have only one employee.

To Find Small Business Support

National Federation of Independent Business (NFIB). Contact this group at 600 Maryland Ave., SW, Suite 700, Washington, DC 20024. The organization supplies research information, publishes a most useful magazine, and offers strong lobbying on behalf of small business issues. It's well worth the $75 per year to join.

U.S. Small Business Administration Service Corps of Executives (SCORE). This agency provides counseling, training, and information. Check your phone directory blue pages under U.S. Goverment, or call 202-653-6279.

The *Steve Bursten, Bootstrap Entrepreneur* ™ *Newsletter* Can Help You Grow
Your Business and Grow Your Profits

Growth is the essence of entrepreneuring. You'll grow your business better and faster with the know-how you need when you subscribe. Six times a year you'll find columns such as "Customers First"—finding and keeping the people who pay your paycheck; "Gross Is Beautiful"—tips to increase your beautiful gross profit; and "The Expense Fighter," among others. You'll also learn from letters and case studies from people just like you. They are making a small business a bigger business, and you can, too.

Your profit guarantee: If after reviewing two issues you're not convinced your earnings will be hundreds to even thousands of dollars higher your first and every year you subscribe, we will cheerfully refund your payment of only $39.00.

Mention this book and receive *free* a $9.95 audiocassette, "Your Business: Make It Fun, Make It Profit!"